OTHER PEOPLE'S MONEY

And How the Bankers Use It

AMERICAN PERSPECTIVES

EDITED BY BERNARD WISHY AND
WILLIAM E. LEUCHTENBURG

ADAMS, JOHN & DANIEL LEONARD: *The American Colonial Crisis: *The John Adams–Daniel Leonard Letters to the Press, 1774–1775*, edited by Bernard Mason

ARNOLD, MATTHEW: *Civilisation in the United States and other writings, edited by Warren Susman

BAKER, RAY STANNARD: Following the Color Line: *American Negro Citizenship in the Progressive Era*, edited by Dewey W. Grantham, Jr. TB/3053

BERMAN, HYMAN (ed.): *The Rise of American Labor: *A Reader*

BOURNE, RANDOLPH S.: War and the Intellectuals: *Collected Essays, 1915–1919*, edited by Carl Resek. TB/3043

BRANDEIS, LOUIS D.: Other People's Money, edited by Richard M. Abrams. TB/3081

BROOKS, VAN WYCK: The Wine of the Puritans and other early writings, edited by Claire Sprague. TB/3082

BURKE, EDMUND: On the American Revolution: *Selected Speeches and Letters*, edited by Elliott Robert Barkan. TB/3068

CAIRNES, J. E.: *The Slave Power, edited by Harold Woodman

FOX, DIXON RYAN: The Decline of Aristocracy in the Politics of New York, 1801–1840, edited by Robert V. Remini. TB/3064

FREEHLING, WILLIAM W., (ed.): *The Nullification Crisis: *A Documentary Record*

GILMAN, CHARLOTTE PERKINS: Women and Economics: *A Study of the Economic Relation Between Men and Women as a Factor in Social Evolution*, edited by Carl N. Degler. TB/3073

HAMILTON, ALEXANDER: The Reports of Alexander Hamilton, edited by Jacob E. Cooke. TB/3060

HUNDLEY, DANIEL R.: *Social Relations in our Southern States, edited by William R. Taylor

HUNTER, ROBERT: Poverty: *Social Conscience in the Progressive Era*, edited by Peter d'A. Jones. TB/3065

HUTCHISON, WILLIAM R. (ed.): *Protestant Liberalism and American Culture since the Civil War: *A Reader*

JACKSON, HELEN HUNT: A Century of Dishonor: *The Early Crusade for Indian Reform*, edited by Andrew F. Rolle. TB/3063

JEFFERSON, THOMAS: Notes on the State of Virginia, edited by Thomas P. Abernethy. TB/3052

LANKFORD, JOHN (ed.): *Captain John Smith's Virginia: *Selections from His Writings*

LIBBY, O. G.: *The Geographical Distribution of the Vote of the Thirteen States on the Federal Constitution: 1787–1788, edited by Lee Benson

MCLOUGHLIN, WILLIAM G. (ed.): *The American Evangelicals: *A Reader*

OSOFSKY, GILBERT (ed.): *Three Slave Narratives

PARTON, JAMES: The Presidency of Andrew Jackson, from the "Life of Jackson," edited by Robert V. Remini. TB/3080

PIKE, JAMES S.: *The Prostrate State: *South Carolina under Negro Government*, edited by Robert F. Durden

RAUSCHENBUSCH, WALTER: Christianity and the Social Crisis, edited by Robert D. Cross. TB/3059

REID, WHITELAW: After the War: *A Tour of the Southern States, 1865–1866*, edited by C. Vann Woodward. TB/3066

RHODES, JAMES FORD: *The Coming of the Civil War (Vol. I); The Civil War (Vol. II): an abridgment of "The History of the United States from the Compromise of 1850," edited by Grady McWhiney

RIIS, JACOB: The Making of an American, edited by Roy Lubove. TB/3070

SHINN, CHARLES HOWARD: Mining Camps: *A Study in American Frontier Government*, edited by Rodman Paul. TB/3062

STEFFENS, LINCOLN: *The Struggle for Self-Government, edited by Joel A. Tarr

TARBELL, IDA M.: The History of the Standard Oil Company: *Briefer Version*, edited by David M. Chalmers. TB/3071

TINDALL, GEORGE B. (ed.): A Populist Reader. TB/3069

TOURGEE, ALBION W.: A Fool's Errand: *A Novel of the South during Reconstruction*, edited by George M. Fredrickson. TB/3074

WEYL, WALTER E.: The New Democracy: *An Essay on Certain Political and Economic Tendencies in the United States*, edited by Charles B. Forcey. TB/3042

* in preparation
5/67

OTHER PEOPLE'S MONEY

And How the Bankers Use It

LOUIS D. BRANDEIS

Edited with an Introduction and Notes by
RICHARD M. ABRAMS

HARPER TORCHBOOKS
Harper & Row, Publishers
New York, Evanston, and London

For my wife
MARCIA

OTHER PEOPLE'S MONEY

First HARPER TORCHBOOK edition published 1967
by Harper & Row, Publishers, Incorporated, 49
East 33rd Street, New York, N.Y. 10016.

CONTENTS

INTRODUCTION TO THE TORCHBOOK EDITION

Brandeis and the Ascendancy of Corporate Capitalism

by RICHARD M. ABRAMS

I

In 1904, in an effort to thwart the "demagogues," "agitators," and "socialists" who had been decrying the trusts, John Moody, the conservative Wall Street chronicler and publisher, issued a weighty compendium of industrial statistics which he called *The Truth About the Trusts*. Moody had only contempt for the popular attacks upon "monopoly" (which was what he called business consolidations generally) ; such attacks he regarded as "apiece with the superficial tendency to block all industrial progress, such as for example the adoption of new inventions and labor-saving machinery of all kinds." (p. xix) Curiously, few contemporary "agitators" ever presented anything so sensational as the statistics Moody produced. But Moody evidently believed that if the public knew "the truth about the trusts," it would be less fearful and less hostile. So, with the candor of a man secure in his conviction about the rightness of what he was describing, Moody set out to establish a statistical basis for honest discussion of "The Trust Problem."

Moody listed 318 industrial combinations with a total capital of $7.25 billion, representing 5,300 distinct industrial plants which, he asserted, dominated American manufactures by the end of 1903. These combinations accounted for 40 per cent of the manufacturing capital in the country. Significantly, 236 of the 318 had been organized within the previous six years.[1] What Moody called the seven "Greater Industrial Trusts" (*viz.,* United States Steel, Amalgamated Copper, American Smelting & Refining, American Sugar Refining, Consolidated Tobacco, International Mercantile Marine, and Standard Oil) alone accounted for $2.66 billion, and represented among them over 1,500 distinct plants. Going beyond

---

[1] A more recent scholarly study indicates that during the period 1897–1904, there were 257 combinations involving 4,227 plants. Jesse Markham, "Survey of the Evidence and Findings on Mergers," *Business Concentration and Price Policy,* A Conference of the Universities-National Bureau Committee for Economic Research (Princeton Univ. Press, 1955), p. 157.

the manufacturing sector, Moody analyzed the "Transportation Trusts" (railroads and ship lines) and the "Franchise Trusts" (trolleys, gas, electric, and telephone companies). Altogether, with the Industrial Trusts, Moody calculated 445 active combinations accounting for a total capitalization of $20.4 billion and representing 8,664 original companies.

Moody also made an effort to discover to what extent these combinations controlled their industries and the economy in general. He examined 92 of the consolidations in detail, and concluded that 78 of them controlled 50 per cent or more of their markets, while 26 controlled more than 80 per cent. Yet this was only part of the story. Through interlocking directorates and financial controls, all the Greater Trusts were dominated by one of two groups: the Rockefeller group and the Morgan group. There were other important capitalist groups, such as those of Vanderbilt and Harriman, but in the most important sectors they were usually allied somehow with Morgan or Rockefeller (who dominated most of the lesser consolidations as well).

It is not possible [Moody said] to more than attempt an approximate estimate of the entire Standard Oil industrial, financial and commerial interests of the nation, as their ramifications are so varied and extensive that a clear line of demarcation could not be drawn which would absolutely distinguish the interests which are more or less dominated by them, from those which are not. . . . It is not merely in oil and its allied industries that the Rockefeller interests are dominant. They are the controlling factors in the Copper Trust and the Smelters' Trust, and are also closely identified with the mammoth Tobacco Trust, which now practically encircles the globe . . . In the hundreds of smaller Industrial Trusts, the Rockefeller interests are also conspicuous in many ways. They dominate a variety of minor industries. . . . Even a hasty glance through the pages of this book will show that the different members of the Standard group of financiers are identified with a great many of the prominent Trusts herein described, and it is a well-known fact that their indirect influence is of great importance in many other industrial consolidations. . . .

Coming to the Franchise aggregations, we find that everywhere the Standard Oil influence is most prominent. The Rockefeller interests practically dominate the entire public service aggregations of Greater New York. . . . They are allied in interest with the well-known United Gas Improvement Company of Philadelphia, which is the leading corporation of the famous Philadelphia or Widener-Elkins groups, and which dominates the public utility interests in a number of the largest centres of population in the United States, and in addition controls the lighting interests of a score or more of the smaller American cities.

. . . In the steam railroad field [Moody continued], we find that the Standard Oil interests are one of the conspicuous factors and are steadily increasing their influence there. . . . It is now freely predicted in Wall Street that the next decade will see the Rockefeller interests the single dominating force in the world of railway finance and control.

The great Rockefeller alliances in the railroad and industrial fields are supplemented and welded together, as it were, through the New York city financial interests of the group. Their banking influence is of very great importance, and their ramifications are far-reaching and of great effectiveness. Thus, the Standard Oil chain of banking institutions, headed by the great National City Bank, with a capital and surplus of $40,000,000, and deposits exceeding $200,000,000, includes also the Hanover National Bank, the Second National Bank, the United States Trust Company, the Farmers Loan & Trust Company, the Central Realty Bond & Trust Company and a number of smaller institutions. . . . The Standard interests are also closely allied with the great life insurance companies, such as the Equitable and the Mutual of New York. (pp. 490–491)

Next to the Rockefeller interests were the Morgan interests.

The Great Morgan enterprises in the industrial world are the Steel and Shipping Trusts, the Electrical Supply Trust, the Rubber Trust, and a score or more of smaller aggregations. . . . But it is in the railroad world that the Morgan influence makes its greatest claim for public attention. In Part V. of this book will be found figures indicating that the Morgan group of steam railroad properties embraces over 47,000 miles of line . . . [representing] $2,265,000,-000 . . . [or] nearly 25 per cent of all the group railroad capital of the United States. The Morgan railroad properties are nearly all located in growing sections of the country, and . . . in most cases the lines embraced absolutely dominate certain sections of the country; such as, for instance, the entire South and the great Northwest. (p. 492)

Like the Rockefeller interests, the Morgan group controlled some of the leading banking and insurance institutions, including the First National Bank, the Chase National Bank, and New York Life.

Moody's tale of concentration and control was not yet finished:

It should not be supposed, however, that these two great groups of capitalists and financiers are in any real sense rivals or competitors for power, or that such a thing as "war" exists between them. For, as a matter of fact, they are not only friendly, but they are allied to each other by many close ties, and it would probably require only a little stretch of the imagination to describe them as a single great Rockefeller-Morgan group. It is felt and recognized on every hand in Wall Street to-day, that they are harmonious in nearly all particulars. . . . (pp. 492–493)

After *The Truth About the Trusts,* one might well wonder what there was left to reveal about the trusts by the Pujo Committee's probe in 1912 into "the Concentration and Control of Money and Credit"—or by Louis Brandeis' summary exposé of "banker exploitation" in *Other People's Money* (1914). Objectively, little had changed in the eight-to-ten year interim. Moody's account was essentially accurate; only his prediction that concentration of industry and finance would continue apace is subject to some correction. For the greatest consolidation movement in American history to date had already ended by the time *The Truth* first reached the bookstores. The only development that might have served to heighten concern about "the trusts" lay in the revelations, growing out of the New York life insurance scandals of 1905–06, about the absorption of the financial resources of the great insurance companies by the great investment banking houses, particularly J. P. Morgan & Company. But even this Moody had already noted; Morgan's position of advantage with life insurance resources had begun at least as early as 1901 when George W. Perkins, Vice-President of New York Life, accepted a partnership with Morgan.

In brief, the facts were substantially the same. But a striking difference in tone, purpose, and anticipated response separates *The Truth About the Trusts* from *Other People's Money.* In part, Moody's obliviousness to the already widespread concern over the concentration of financial power suggests what a narrow segment of "the public" he appears to have been addressing—a public of investors, bankers, and brokers. On the other hand, the attitude implicit in his approach also suggests the validity of one of the more perceptive contemporary observations about the progressive movement—that so much of what the movement condemned had only recently been generally accepted and even honored.[2] Moody's confident justification of "monopolies" rested primarily on his belief that they grew "from customs and ethical standards which have for a long time been recognized as fair and equitable among an apparent majority of our citizens." (p. 500) In 1904, it was still

[2] Walter Lippmann, *Drift and Mastery* (Mitchell Kennerly, 1914), pp. 5–9.

reasonable to believe (even mistakenly) that the public on the whole approved the performance of consolidated corporate enterprise.

Few would dispute the contention that the trusts, though they represented a vital organizational innovation in business techniques, brought about no radical change in business "customs and ethical standards." The most critical might say, with the caustic Thorstein Veblen, that the trusts were indeed only "the self-acting collusive storekeeper and banker of the nineteenth century country town" writ large—that "the same stock of men with the same traditions and ideals [were] doing Big Business on the same general plan."[3] Historian Ralph Hidy explains the industrial magnates' behavior more sympathetically as simply the product "of the ideas that men lived by in the dynamic, democratic society of the time," noting especially that, in economic matters, the ideas of farmers and small businessmen seemed dominant.[4]

The antitrust debate itself only reaffirmed the conventional business outlook. Economists especially are struck by how little of the contemporary debate touched on the principle of profit-oriented business enterprise, or even raised questions about increased consumer costs deriving from noncompetitive high prices, market quotas, and restricted output. American antitrust attention focused rather on the way in which the trusts subverted the American social system based on small proprietary units of business enterprise and thus threatened "the rights of the common man in business."[5]

That the trusts subverted the American business system by driving out the independent proprietor, and that they undermined democratic political institutions through the force of overbearing and corrupting economic power, were both appealing arguments. But at the turn of the century it would seem that they were still not so appealing as the counterargument, almost uncontested, that the trusts were responsible for America's huge economic success and that business consolidations would be the instrument of American ascendancy throughout the world. The consolidationist promise of economic abundance and national power was all the more

---

[3] From *Absentee Ownership and Business Enterprise in Recent Times* (Huebsch, 1923).

[4] See "Some Implications of the Recent Literature on the History of the Petroleum Industry: A Review Article," *Business History Review,* XXX (Sept. 1956), 332–333.

[5] See W. E. Baldwin, *Antitrust and the Changing Corporation* (Duke Univ. Press, 1961), pp. 29–33; Hans Thorelli, *The Federal Antitrust Policy* (Stockholm, 1955), p. 227; John H. Bunzel, *The American Small Businessman* (Knopf, 1962), *passim.*

appealing because by 1904 it had the appearance of having been
already largely fulfilled. Who at the time doubted that America
was fast becoming, if it was not already, the richest nation in the
world? Who, even among the anti-imperialists of the day, was
willing to deny that overseas markets and resources were or would
soon be indispensable for continued economic growth? Who would
deny that "the trusts" were our best weapon in international business competition? And who would willingly risk killing the goose
that nearly everyone agreed had laid the golden egg? "We want
to be provided with things abundantly and cheaply," said William
Graham Sumner; "that means that we want increased economic
power. All these enterprises are efforts to satisfy that want, and
they promise to do it." "Are we prepared," Sumner asked, "to give
up the comforts of civilization rather than continue to pay the price
of them?"[6] The answer was, quite evidently, No. Thus John
Moody could conclude with complete confidence: "Whether one
may regard monopoly as a curse or a blessing it is too deeply rooted
in civilized society to be whisked away with a broom. This being
so, there would seem to be no immediate prospect of 'effective' legislation touching the Trust problem." (p. 501)

By 1913, when Louis Brandeis began writing *Other People's
Money,* the prospects for "effective legislation" aimed at restraining
corporate power seemed more auspicious. In the intervening years,
although concentration had not increased significantly, much had
happened to suggest to the public (1) that the aggregations of
wealth and power in corporate consolidations were not entirely
the result of "natural" forces presumed indispensable to civilization;
(2) that the obnoxious features of corporate organization might
indeed outweigh the advantageous; and (3) that opposition to the
further growth of corporate power was not necessarily futile.
Among other things, Theodore Roosevelt had made gestures of
throwing the prestige of the presidency behind the effort to "bust
the trusts"; in spite of T.R.'s belief that business consolidations
were generally beneficent as well as inevitable, his administration
revived expectations that the Sherman Act could be used effectively
against monopolistic practices. In successfully prosecuting Swift
& Company for attempting to fix prices in the meat packing industry in 1905, the Justice Department had gotten the Supreme
Court to rescind the "hands off" policy adopted in the E. C. Knight

[6] From "The Concentration of Wealth: Its Economic Justification," in
The Essays of William Graham Sumner (Yale Univ. Press, 1934), II, p. 166;
and "Another Chapter on Monopoly," *The Independent* (March 15, 1888).

("Sugar Trust") case of 1895. In addition, muckraking efforts such as *Frenzied Finance* (1905)—Thomas W. Lawson's confessions of a Wall Street operator—though self-serving and unreliable, had helped to confirm some of the darkest suspicions about the new-fangled finance capitalism. Following the "banker's panic" of 1907, moreover, the creation of the National Monetary Commission had revived for the first time since the Populist era widespread discussion of banking reform, with an emphasis on more orderly and centralized control of banking practices. Meanwhile, insurgents within the Republican party, especially in the midwest, had struck upon the trust issue (among others) at least partly as a lever to loosen the grip of the eastern wing of the party; by joining the Bryan Democrats in charging that industrial and financial power was concentrated in the northeastern corner of the nation to the disadvantage of America's "heartland," they gave antitrust the stature of a bipartisan progressive cause. Finally, the Supreme Court's decision in 1911 that Standard Oil and the "Tobacco Trust" had acted in *unreasonable* restraint of trade threw wide open the whole issue of how, and what, policy should be made on business concentration.

Neither antitrusters nor consolidationists were entirely happy with "the Rule of Reason" enunciated in the Standard Oil decision. The new doctrine satisfied some of the objections among corporate leaders that the Sherman Act, if enforced literally, would create chaos in the business community. "The Supreme Court," said New York Senator Chauncey Depew (who was also Board Chairman of the New York Central Railroad), "has rendered a decision which has swept the platform out from under [the antitrust insurgents], and made the constitution good for another 125 years. The great decision says that every trade combination in the United States which may be regarded as unlawful must be judged by the light of reason."[7] Yet the decision also left business leaders uncertain about which practices were "reasonable" and which would be subject to costly litigation.

On the other hand, the doctrine outraged those for whom the Sherman Act represented a deliberate policy decision by Congress, expressing the public's will, aimed specifically against *all* combinations, agreements, or conspiracies which effectively reduced competition and impaired the economic processes of the free market.

[7] Speech to the U.S. Chamber of Commerce in Paris, July 4, 1911, in Depew, *Speeches and Addresses on the Threshold of Eighty* (Privately printed, New York, 1915), p. 130.

"When Congress prohibited *every* contract, combination, or conspiracy in restraint of commerce," Justice Harlan declared in his separate opinion on the Standard Oil case,

> it prescribed a simple, definite rule that all could understand. . . . Congress, in effect, said that there should be *no* restraint of trade, *in any form,* and this court solemnly adjudged many years ago [in U.S. v. Trans-Missouri Freight Assn., 1897, and in the Northern Securities case, 1903] that Congress meant what it thus said in clear and explicit words of an act. But those who condemn the action of Congress are now, in effect, informed that the Courts will allow such restraints of interstate commerce as are shown not to be unreasonable or undue.

Harlan in fact had written the majority opinion in the Northern Securities case, in which he had asserted: "The [Sherman] Act is not limited to restraints of interstate and international trade or commerce that are unreasonable in their nature, but embraces all direct restraints, reasonable or unreasonable, imposed by any combination, conspiracy or monopoly upon such trade or commerce." In more modern parlance, Harlan was insisting that *Congress had decided* that the test of violation did not lie in the social or economic *performance* of a combination (i.e., whether such performance was deemed beneficial or pernicious), but in the *fact* of impaired competition.

At least twice, congressional action appeared to reaffirm that decision. In 1908, the U.S. Senate Committee on Interstate Commerce had pointedly rejected a bill that would have permitted the I.C.C. or the Bureau of Corporations to pass upon the "reasonableness" of specific business agreements or consolidations that would reduce competition:

> The [Sherman] Act as it exists is clear, comprehensive, certain and highly remedial. . . . To destroy or undermine it at the present juncture, when combinations are on the increase, and appear to be as oblivious as ever of the rights of the public, would be a calamity.[8]

In 1913, after the enunciation of the "Rule of Reason," a Senate Committee again asserted its opposition to "exceptions" from the proscriptions of the Sherman Act, and berated the Supreme Court for taking policy-making powers into its own hands:

> It is inconceivable [declared the Committee] that in a country governed by a written Constitution and statute law the courts can be permitted to test each restraint of trade by the economic standard

[8] Senate Report 848, 60th Congress, 2d Session, pp. 8–11.

which the individual members of the court may happen to approve. . . . We [should soon] cease to be a Government of law and become a Government of men, and, moreover, of a very few men, and they appointed by the President.[9]

In appearance, then, the stage seemed set in 1913 for a showdown on the trust issue; for perhaps the only time in the course of the nation's history the American public seemed on the brink of a momentous decision about its social and economic order. The presidential campaign of 1912 itself had focused largely on the conflict between alternative policies of acceptance of great corporate combinations under Federal regulatory supervision (Theodore Roosevelt's New Nationalism), and the restoration of small unit business competition by means of reinvigorated antitrust laws (Woodrow Wilson's New Freedom). Wilson's victory placed in the White House a man explicitly committed to a program designed to restore small business (and even small town) enterprise to its central role in America. "I am going to think of towns such as I have seen in Indiana," Wilson had declared, "towns of the old American pattern," free from the control of great absentee corporations. "My thought is going to be bent upon the prevention of the concentration of industry in this country upon such a scale" as to subvert the independence of such towns; America's unborn children must not "open their eyes in a country where they must be employees or nothing, in a land of merely regulated monopoly, where all the conditions of industry are determined by small groups of men."[10]

In fact, in the ensuing contest between Congress and the Court for control over national policy the Court quickly demonstrated its superiority. The Court's triumph derived from the greater consistency and continuity of its thought and purpose—due in part to qualities inherent in the judiciary, but also in part to the determination of specific members on the bench. Congress and the Executive, on the other hand, gave only fitful attention to the issue; they remained profoundly uncertain of their purposes and tended to divide sharply over specific proposals; and when they acted at all, they typically "split the difference" on an issue for which compromise could only mean failure. Every statutory equivocation, every ambiguity of phrase, every modifier, hedge, and accommodation said to the Court, in effect, "*You* make the decision"—and it did.

[9] Senate Report 1326, 62d Congress, 3d Session, p. 17.
[10] *The New Freedom* (Prentice-Hall edition, 1961), pp. 166–167.

Doomed to failure by the force of social and economic inertia, the willful determination of the courts, and the fecklessness of Wilson's own leadership, the New Freedom nevertheless represented a last brave effort to avert the triumph of "corporate America" and to renew the vigor of American small business enterprise. That those who carried on the effort in subsequent times have come typically to be characterized as "Brandeisians" suggests the vital role that Louis Dembitz Brandeis played in shaping that feature of the New Freedom.

II

Brandeis first met Woodrow Wilson on August 28, 1912, when Wilson was still searching for an effective campaign formula to rival Roosevelt's New Nationalism. Until that time, Wilson had clung stolidly to the tariff issue while his campaign sagged under the weight of time-worn banalities. Brandeis suggested to Wilson that he focus his campaign on Roosevelt's apparent alliance with "big business" by distinguishing carefully between T.R.'s program of "regulated monopoly"—i.e., a program that accepted consolidated business while trying to force "the trusts" to be good— and a program that denied monopoly even tacit legitimacy, seeking instead to "regulate competition" toward the end of precluding the conditions conducive to monopolistic power. Wilson's own thinking on the subject seems to have been ambivalent at the time, but Brandeis' suggestions apparently stimulated certain of Wilson's strong traditionalist preferences while also touching a political nerve. Although as late as 1907 Wilson had publicly criticized those who failed to see the advantages of consolidated business enterprise, by the end of August 1912 he was unequivocally emphasizing the virtues of decentralization and a supervised free market.

At the time that Brandeis received Wilson's invitation for campaign advice that August, he was 56 years old (exactly Wilson's age) and a millionaire who had virtually retired from a successful corporate law career in order to offer his legal skills to those attempting to fight corporate arrogance. He had already gained national renown as "the People's Attorney," having led battles for more than a decade against corporate power in Massachusetts and, after 1908, on the national scene as well. As a founder of the Massachusetts Public Franchise League at the turn of the century, Brandeis had helped fight to a standstill the "traction trusts" and the "gas interests" which, with the backing of New York and Boston investment bankers, had sought to consolidate and control the vital service industries in the state. He had forced the Boston gas companies to accept a "sliding scale" price-and-dividend system whereby dividends could be increased only when gas rates were reduced. He had struggled to keep Massachusetts from relaxing its control of corporate finance in emulation of New Jersey, Delaware, and the newer states to the West. Aroused by the life insurance scandals in New York, but even more by the inefficiency reflected in the high cost of life insurance obtainable through the private companies, he had persuaded the Massachusetts legislature to permit the sale by savings banks of small denomination life insurance policies, to be paid for in small weekly or monthly installments, for the benefit of low income families.

In 1908, with the assistance of his sister-in-law, Josephine Goldmark, and the National Consumers' League, he had prepared the precedent-setting law brief which persuaded the Supreme Court to uphold Oregon's curbs on the hours of factory labor for women— a triumph for the new "sociological jurisprudence." (*Muller v. Oregon.*) Meanwhile, his unsuccessful efforts, beginning in 1906, to block the monopolization of New England's transportation system by J. P. Morgan's New Haven Railroad had brought to Brandeis intimate experience in the ways and means of the new financial oligarchy—its deceptiveness, its ruthlessness, and its power. His fight attracted national attention, and brought him an invitation from Robert LaFollette, the maverick Republican Senator from Wisconsin, to serve as LaFollette's close advisor on national antitrust legislation.

Brandeis became a figure of national renown in 1910 through three separate activities. In January of that year, Robert Collier and Norman Hapgood of *Collier's Magazine* brought him to Washington to serve as counsel for the magazine and for Louis Glavis, an Interior Department subordinate who had been dismissed for publicly accusing Secretary of the Interior Richard Ballinger of complicity in a conspiracy among financial magnates to defraud the public of thousands of acres of public lands. In the congressional hearings on the charges, Brandeis scandalized the country by exposing the premature official whitewash of Ballinger and by catching both the Attorney General and the President of the United States in an out-right lie; President Taft and Attorney General George Wickersham were compelled to confess that they had deliberately predated a report so as to make it appear that Taft had carefully studied the controversy before firing Glavis, although in fact Taft had merely accepted Ballinger's account of the entire dispute.

In August of the same year Brandeis accepted the chairmanship of a mediation committee to help settle a massive and disorderly strike in the New York garment industry. It was in the course of that work that Brandeis introduced the idea of the "preferential union shop" as an alternative to the irreconcilable demands of union leaders for a closed shop and those of employers for open-shop control of their labor force. In the union shop, an employee was expected to join the union some time after being hired. That proposal, as well as the establishment of permanent conciliation and arbitration machinery which Brandeis, Louis Marshall, Meyer London, and Henry Moskowitz had incorporated into the "Protocol of Peace" for the New York garment industry, served as important precedents for future labor negotiations throughout the country.

That same summer and fall, Brandeis introduced to the public essentially for the first time the principles of "scientific management." While serving as counsel for the Boston Chamber of Commerce in hearings before the I.C.C. on a proposed railroad rate increase for shipments east of the Mississippi, Brandeis presented a tightly-argued brief against the rairoads' (and railroad brother-hoods') contentions that increased labor and materials costs had necessitated a rate rise. Throughout the course of the hearings, Brandeis conferred closely with Frederick W. Taylor, H. L. Gantt, F. B. Gilbreth, and other founders of the scientific management movement. Their contention was that time and motion studies, proper cost accounting methods, and the reestablishment of competitive buying from the railroads' suppliers (such as the steel manufacturers) could reduce costs and make the solicited rate advance unnecessary.

In his argument during the Eastern Rate Case hearings, Brandeis touched directly on one of the themes that he developed in *Other People's Money:* Why, he asked, had not the railroads devoted as much cooperative energy toward resisting the rise of steel prices as they were then devoting toward raising rates? The answer, Brandeis asserted, lay in the interlocking directorates of the steel and railroad companies, and in the control of both industries by the same financial interests. He pointed out that 40 of the 65 directors of the steel companies were also on the boards of the railroads. "If the interests of the railroads are to be looked after and to be protected," he asked, "how can you hope to get full protection when the man who ought to protect the railroads is in a position which is necessarily not a disinterested one?"

He went on to make a second point that later appeared at the heart of the argument in *Other People's Money:*

> Everyone has called attention to this fact, that while the great systems—I mean great in mileage and great in earnings—have been suffering from increased operating expenses, certain . . . [smaller railroads] have shown a tendency to greater net returns and prosperity. Is that a fact of significance? I ask the Commission to consider whether there is not a causal connection between the fact of bigness, the fact of this extraordinary gross, and the fact of reduced net; whether it is not a fact that the Pennsylvania System, and the New York Central System, and . . . the Baltimore & Ohio System have not exceeded what may be called the limit of greatest efficiency, . . . where by reason of the multiplicity of problems and the distance of the circumference, looseness of administration arises that overcomes any advantage from size, overcomes it so far as to make it a relatively losing proposition.

In effect, Brandeis was arguing that many of the major railroads were simply too large to be run efficiently and that, moreover, if only the railroads had had the proper, institutionally-induced incentives for cost reductions, they would not have needed rate advances to maintain their net earnings. Instead of using their collective power and the tools of science to increase operating efficiency, the railroads, their financial rulers, their associates among their suppliers, and their allies in the railroad-worker brotherhoods, simply coalesced in the attempt to exact higher prices across the board from shippers and the public, and to split the receipts among them.

It was a sign of the times rather than of the power of Brandeis' persuasion that the railroads lost their plea. The I.C.C. declined to adopt Brandeis' proposals, partly because of labor unions' strenuous objections that scientific management would lead the way to abuses of the labor force. Nevertheless, it ruled against an advance in freight rates, arguing simply that railroad earnings were already high enough. Without the benefit of the Brandeisian analysis, the decision lacked logical coherence; it seemed to reflect merely the current shift of political influence away from the industrial titans centered around the railroad industry to the merchant and shipping interests.

All the same, for Brandeis the decision served a sufficient purpose. It was, he declared, a great "victory for conservatism." "It will tend to convince the people," he wrote, "that there is power in our government to create a body which can successfully resist the demands of great corporations, and it must therefore tend to allay not only hostility and suspicion, but the demand for government ownership of national monopolies."[11] The toast to conservatism was no rhetorical or tactical gesture. Although Brandeis' hostility to corporate finance capitalism gave him the aspect of a radical, his animus in fact derived from deeply conservative preferences, both personal and economic. Corporate consolidation represented to him an ominous challenge to individualism, while corporate truculence, which business concentration tended to encourage, enhanced the logic and potency of popular demands for a socialist solution to industrial problems. For, as Brandeis saw it, if one accepted consolidation, not only did it become logically difficult to justify privately-owned and operated enterprise in a democratic society, but it also became politically difficult to resist pressures for public ownership. If Brandeis seemed to be fighting the corporations more than he fought the socialists, it was only because he believed that socialism would come less from the efforts of the socialists than from the blunders of the corporate leaders and their consolidationist allies.

What real radicalism there was in Brandeis seemed to have grown out of an increasing sense of outrage directed not even so much against the new economic modes that he believed threatened fundamental American ideals, as against those in positions of power who he believed compromised their integrity by making disingenuous accommodations to the new and pernicious economic order. The Ballinger affair and Brandeis' role in contributing to the anti-Taft insurgency that split the G.O.P. help to illustrate this point. Brandeis had voted for Taft in 1908; he had thought him "admirably qualified for the position" of President (though he feared "the moneybags" in the Republican party might run riot because of the Democrats' evident weakness).[12] On the issue of business concentration, Taft's Administration performed in almost "Brandeisian" fashion, and it remains an historical irony that the break between Taft and Roosevelt, the touted trust-buster, finally came over Taft's decision to use the Sherman Act against the United States Steel Corporation despite T.R.'s bitter objections. Brandeis' estrangement from Taft grew from more subtle sources;

[11] "A Victory for Conservatism," *Moody's Magazine*, March 1911; quoted in Alpheus T. Mason, *Brandeis, A Free Man's Life* (Viking, 1946), p. 334.
[12] To Alfred Brandeis, Nov. 4, 1908. Louis D. Brandeis Manuscript Collection, Law Library, University of Louisville, Louisville, Kentucky.

in particular, that Taft had come to represent a style of politics and social behavior that manifested much of what was wrong with the "old guard" generally: a slavish insistence upon the presumed dictates of precedent, a rigid formality of thought, a willful blindness to new social needs, a disingenuousness of manner, and above all a devotion to group loyalties that too often transcended public responsibilities and even simple honesty. Brandeis had come into the Ballinger affair from a commitment to the conservation policies inaugurated by Roosevelt and Gifford Pinchot; he had been persuaded that Secretary of the Interior Richard Ballinger had conspired to "give away" to "the Guggenheim interests" some vital coal deposits in the public domain. But it was the deliberate deceptiveness of Taft and his chief aides, the automatic and unquestioning support that Taft and the old guard leaders rendered Ballinger against the "outsiders" who challenged him, that soon came to impress Brandeis as *the* issue.

In many ways, the issue of group loyalty symbolized the crux of the conflict between progressive and old guard on the antitrust controversy as well. For in the long run, policy toward "the trusts" came to be shaped not so much by legislative action (which ostensibly was designed to prevent concentration) or by the "better judgment" of conservatives like Taft (who genuinely distrusted the growing concentration of corporate power) as by the willingness of men in power like Taft and the Supreme Court justices to repress their otherwise tenacious commitment to traditional American modes in favor of loyalty to their colleagues in power whose fortunes and energies were tied up with the revolutionary corporate practices in question. It is difficult to explain in any other way the judicial and administrative sleight of hand which effectively revolutionized corporate law in the last half of the nineteenth and early twentieth century.

Brandeis tended to view himself, with some good reason, as working within the policy-making councils of the nation. And yet, he never acquired the instinct for group loyalty that appears to have governed so much of the behavior of the country's policy makers. Apparently he had always been outraged by "the wickedness of people, shielding wrong doers, and passing them off (or at least allowing them to pass themselves off) as honest men." (To Alice Goldmark Brandeis, February 2, 1891.) Not even family loyalty could dissuade him from what he regarded as his duty. When his brother Alfred suggested that in his assault on the Taft Administration Brandeis try to keep from implicating Charles

Nagel, Taft's Secretary of Commerce who was also their once
fondly-regarded brother-in-law, he refused in a rather typical
though stiff and even pompous fashion:

> Your remarks [he wrote] are entirely pertinent but I think not
> sound. There is nothing for me to do but to follow the trail of evil
> wherever it extends. *Fiat Iustitia.* In the fight against special interest
> we shall receive no quarter and may as well make up our minds to
> give none. Every attempt to [be merciful] . . . with the special
> interests *during the fight* simply results in their taking advantage of
> the merciful. I think Wickersham and his acts are a fair sample
> of [what] . . . Wall Street and high finance make of a finely gifted
> and no doubt originally honorable man.

Their brother-in-law, he implied might as easily be corrupted.[13]
(Hadn't Charles once remarked to Louis how difficult it was "to
differ from the men with whom you are accustomed to go"?)[14]

Brandeis' lack of group loyalty probably was due to the fact
that he never really made it "in." There is a small irony in this,
as there is in the role of maverick in which he found himself cast
after the turn of the century. For, during almost the first fifty
years of his life, Louis Brandeis spoke and behaved unselfcon-
sciously as if he were unquestionably one among the custodians of
American culture. He could speak of "the American ideal" and of
"our heritage" without any seeming ambiguities and could freely
use the word "unAmerican," even as late as 1910, to describe, for
example, closed-shop labor unionism. (He had said he would not
participate in the Garment Strike negotiations that year if the closed
shop issue were to be included in the bargaining.) He assumed
there was an essential coherence to the "American tradition," and
that there were eternal moral truths bound up in it. He believed in
the mission implied in the American promise of liberty, equality,
and justice for all, regardless of class, though, in the fashion of
much late nineteenth century thought he tended to read America
as New England, to view New England's tradition as the nation's.
And (more to the point) as that tradition seemed increasingly
subjected to the challenges of modern industrialism and massive
immigration, he came to stress the impelling need for cultural unity.
"Habits of living or of thought," he declared in 1905, "which tend
to keep alive differences of origin or to classify men according to
their religious beliefs are inconsistent with the American ideal of

[13] To Alfred, May 1, 1910.
[14] Quoted in Mason, *Brandeis: A Free Man's Life,* p. 290.

brotherhood, and are disloyal."[15] It was on behalf of "the American ideal" that Brandeis came to devote his energies to civic reform. As he put it in 1903, he feared "lest the great heritage of an honorable, glorious past, handed down to us by our fathers," be dissipated by revolutionary and dishonest business practices, boodling politicians, and radical unionism.[16]

For this Louisville-born son of Jewish-Bohemian immigrants to have reminded Bostonians of the great heritage handed down by "our fathers" may have struck some of his listeners as presumptuous. If so, Brandeis remained for the time quite unaware of it. He had adopted Boston as his own, had acquired a New England quality in his speech, and had gained entrance into a few of the better country and polo clubs in the community; these achievements, so far as he was concerned, had been sufficient to make him "a Bostonian." It was not until he reached the half-century mark that he was rudely reminded of his "outsider" status. A victim of vulgar anti-Semitic attacks, which began during the years of his fight against the New Haven Railroad's management, Brandeis discovered that being a Jew was no more a matter of choice than acceptance into "the Establishment" was an automatic consequence of fidelity to the American consensus.

Brandeis had never especially regarded himself as Jewish, though he had never denied his Jewishness either. His family seems to have derived from a post-emancipation Jewish sect called "ex-Frankists" (from the erstwhile followers of a heretic eighteenth century Jew who lost his following when he adopted Roman Catholicism), so that even in Prague, before its emigration to Kentucky in 1849, the Brandeis family was decidedly on the periphery of Jewish community life. Aside from a nostalgic fondness for an uncle, Lewis Dembitz, who late in life became a well-known Jewish scholar and for whom Brandeis changed his middle name from "David" to "Dembitz," there seems little that was specifically Jewish in his life. The Germanness of his affinities and associations, especially in his early manhood, is far more evident; as a youth he studied at the German and English Academy of Louisville, and later at both the University of Vienna and the Annen-Realschule in Dresden. His well-kept financial records show no

[15] "What Loyalty Demands," speech to the Boston Century Club, November 28, 1905. Brandeis repeated these sentiments in an interview for the *Boston Jewish Advocate,* Dec. 9, 1910.
[16] *Boston Herald,* April 9, 1903; also quoted in A. T. Mason, *Brandeis: Lawyer and Judge in the Modern State* (Princeton Univ. Press, 1933), p. 23.

special gifts to Jewish philanthropies before 1905, and some members of his immediate family married non-Jews evidently without causing any domestic stir; he and his wife were themselves married at home by Felix Adler, his wife's uncle and the founder of the quasi-religious Ethical Culture Society. Nevertheless, as Brandeis pointedly remarked some years later, "It is the non-Jews who create . . . disabilities [for the Jews] and in so doing give definition to the term Jew. These disabilities . . . do not end with a renunciation of faith, however sincere."[17] By 1913, Brandeis was an ardent Zionist telling audiences how "practical experience" had convinced him that "to be good Americans, we must be better Jews, and to be better Jews, we must become Zionists." *Now* when he spoke of "our fathers" it was in reference to those who in ancient times had laid claim to Palestine as the Jewish "fatherland."[18]

Brandeis' conversion to Zionism represented no fundamental shift in his values and only a partial change in his view of "the American ideal." If Brandeis had once tended to view America as New England, he came to regard Jewishness very much the same way. The same New England attributes he had exalted in the American tradition he now picked out of Judaism: Jews had a stern sense of duty, just as the Puritans had; they revelled in intellectual achievements, just as the Puritans had; they respected leadership while remaining strongly individualistic; and—once more like the Puritans—they had a keenly developed sense of community responsibility. "I find Jews possessed of those very qualities which we of the twentieth century seek to develop in our struggle for justice and democracy; a deep moral feeling which makes them capable of noble acts; a deep sense of the brotherhood of man; and a high intelligence, the fruit of three thousand years of civilization."[19] Indeed, as Brandeis came to see it, Zionism represented "in Jewish life what Progressivism does in general American life."[20]

Brandeis' affinity for the New England tradition was reflected in his personal life. He possessed a real "Puritan streak." It impelled him to standards of excellence that went beyond the reach of ordinary effort, even as it made paramount virtues of simplicity and self-reliance as life styles. It left him impressed by the power

[17] "The Jewish Problem, How to Solve It," an address first given in June, 1915 before a Conference of the Eastern council of Reform Rabbis; printed in *Brandeis on Zionism*, ed. by Felix Frankfurter (Zionist Organization of America, 1942), p. 14.
[18] Quoted in Mason, *Brandeis: A Free Man's Life*, pp. 445–446, 447.
[19] Quoted in Mason, *Ibid.*, p. 445.
[20] To Jacob Billikopf, June 16, 1916.

and pervasiveness of natural forces yet insistent upon the responsibility of men for their own individual predicaments. It led him to regard work, and especially struggle, as the principal builders of strong character and the vehicles of personal salvation. It made him confident of the knowledge of morality, and suspicious of changes that seemed to threaten the institutional bases of character and manliness.

Throughout his life Brandeis lived simply, almost self-consciously so. His clothes and his living quarters, even after his appointment to the Supreme Court, were plain, suggesting orderliness and frugality. He avoided spectator entertainment, believing it weakened one's incentives toward self-reliance. According to one story, Jane Addams had to persuade him that radio and the movies had at least the redeeming qualities of providing welcome relief to the humdrum existence of most working people.[21] He brought sandwiches from home for lunch at his office. And it is said that when the new Supreme Court building was completed he refused to occupy his new office because the suite seemed too elegant for the austere labor that justice required of him. Personally, he seems to have been warm and gregarious among intimates but somewhat distant and exacting of others. "Even Brandeis would have approved that," became a standard comment among the members of his former law firm about a job meticulously done.[22] He must have known that he sometimes appeared captious, but it did not seriously disturb him. "You often said, dearest mother, that I find fault," he wrote in 1888. "I always told you candidly that I felt and sought to change only that little which appeared to me possible of improvement."

Despite his simplicity, his Puritan strain included a strong element of ambition. After graduating from Harvard Law School in 1878, he was persuaded by Charles Nagel and his sister Fannie to begin his law career with them in St. Louis. But St. Louis displeased him because of its intellectual vacuousness and social frivolity. "Dancing three nights out of six," he expostulated to his sister Amy only months after his arrival there; such a "dose of dancing" led him to melancholia "and to moralize on the total depravity of man and woman."[23] The thought of being buried alive in that outpost of civilization appalled him, and he brooded about

[21] Norman Hapgood, *The Changing Years* (Farrar & Rinehart, 1933), p. 199.
[22] Mason, *Brandeis: A Free Man's Life,* p. 86.
[23] *Ibid.,* p. 54.

the possibility of missing "the tide in the affairs of men/Which, taken at the flood, leads on to fortune." (Brandeis copied these familiar lines from Shakespeare's *Julius Caesar* into his notebook early in 1879.) By July 1879, he was back in Boston to stay. To his mother, he confessed his ambition:

> When I received your letter and those of the others, it seems to me as if I were a fool to have settled here so far away, instead of staying with you and enjoying you and your love. Of course one can live anywhere. . . . But man is strange, at least this one is; he does not enjoy what he has—and he always wants what he does not yet have. That probably is called ambition—the delusion, for which one is always ready to offer a sacrifice.[24]

The capitalist spirit thus mixed generously with the Puritan ethic in Brandeis' soul. His Puritanism indeed had a heavy overlay of nineteenth century American darwinist economics. Character, struggle, achievement, efficiency, excellence, and responsibility he typically interpreted in economic terms. Private enterprise was not simply a means of livelihood but a way of life, a character-building endeavor, a source of financial independence, and thereby of personal freedom. His own avowed ambition, chosen early in life, was to achieve an economic success that would leave him self-sufficient, free of the commands and coercions of others. The competitive market place was the arena in which man sharpened his wits, strengthenend his character, achieved self-reliance, and gave expression to his freedom. ". . . Only through the participation by the many in the responsibilities and determinations of business," he once declared, "can Americans secure the moral and intellectual development essential to the maintenance of liberty."[25]

It is in this that one can discover the key to Brandeis' enmity toward corporate capitalism. The corporation for Brandeis was the nemesis of individuality and sound character, for it represented virtually the antithesis of business enterprise itself. Brandeis often drew the battle lines between "the men who are trying to do business" and those who favored the corporations. In a world where private endeavor encountered the legally-privileged collective power of corporate enterprise, where success came from the application of concentrated brute force against even the sharpest wit and the manliest effort, and where wealth and power could

[24] Quoted in Mason, *Brandeis: A Free Man's Life*, pp. 54, 59.
[25] From Brandeis' dissenting opinion in Liggett v. Lee, 288 U. S. 517 (1933).

derive from the exploitation of other people's savings and of
the simple, ingenuous labor it represented, what basis for a noble
civilization remained?

If there was a Brandeisian philosophy, the idea that excellence
developed from *struggle* (or, in economic language, *competition*)
provided its central thought. At least it was a sentiment he expressed more consistently than others. "It is not good for us that
we should lose the fighting quality . . .," he wrote around 1912.
"There is something better than peace and that is the peace that
is won by struggle."[26] At the same time, Brandeis insisted that a
free and orderly society required cultural unity and the kind of
spontaneous cooperation that derives from a shared sense of
commonwealth; he never wholly threw off his early commitment
to social homogeneity. Not even his adoption of the Zionist cause,
for all its pluralist implications, really opened to him the possibilities of cultural diversity as a liberalizing social and political influence or as an instrument for creative energies. As he put it
himself, it was "practical experience" that had led him to Zionism,
not any broader, pluralist considerations,[27] and in fact, he never
adopted Zionism in its complete form as a movement for a Jewish
national and cultural renascence; to Brandeis, especially after 1915
when "loyal Americanism" appeared as an issue of wartime
patriotism, Zionism represented merely the effort to establish a
Jewish haven abroad, with or without the status of national
sovereignty.[28] In sum, despite the pluralist inferences that one
might derive from Brandeis' emphasis on "struggle," and despite
the apparent "hyphenism" suggested by his advocacy of Zionism,
there was actually little of the pluralist in Brandeis. Brandeis'
conception of the role of competition in the shaping of character
and in the restraint of power applied primarily to economics; the

[26] Osmond K. Fraenkel, ed., *The Curse of Bigness: Miscellaneous Papers
of Louis D. Brandeis* (Viking Press, 1934), pp. 45–46.
[27] Nor did Brandeis approach Zionism in a pluralist spirit; once he
espoused the cause, he seems to have required the same absolutistic unity of
American Jews that he earlier had required of Americans generally on
behalf of "Americanism." "Loyalty to America demands," he averred in
1915, "that each American Jew become a Zionist. . . . Every Jew in America must stand up and be counted . . . or prove himself, wittingly or un-
wittingly, of the few who are against their own people." See, "The Jewish
Problem, How to Solve It," pp. 29, 35.
[28] I am indebted especially to Dr. Yonathan Shapiro, of the University of
Tel-Aviv, for this point. His as yet unpublished doctoral dissertation, "Leadership of the American Zionist Organization, 1897–1930," Department of
Sociology, Columbia University, 1964, is a provocative and remarkably fruitful source of information about Brandeis.

great emphasis he placed on business decentralization, indeed, originated most of all from his inability to imagine another source of diversity and contest within a society.

Actually, one must be cautious about taking any Brandeis statement (including those quoted here) entirely literally, or as expressing a part of a complete philosophical viewpoint. As one contemporary observed, it is difficult to discover any general, well-considered system in Brandeis' approach to problems; his books seem simply "an endless collection of facts and a consideration of practical matters."[29] Brandeis generally prided himself on his focus on "practical matters"; in that age of criticism of philosophical systems, "pragmatism" and "instrumentalism" were badges of hard-headed enlightenment. Yet Brandeis' thought (or thoughts) emanated for the most part from a constellation of moral and sentimental preferences (perhaps *prejudices* is not too strong a word) which his emphasis upon "data" tends to obscure. When one examines his arguments for the facts he omitted as well as for those he included, it becomes evident that Brandeis did not always arrive at his position after studying the facts but instead skillfully manipulated the data in order to justify his conventionally-founded preferences. His arguments were always able, fundamentally honest, and generally cogent; they presented invaluable information for challenging complacent conclusions about innumerable sacred cows in American life; but one must not assume that they were built upon a foundation of cool rationality and objectivity.

This is especially important for a discussion of Brandeis' views on business concentration, because Brandeis has had a reputation, among some historians as well as among his contemporaries, for an instrumentalistic disdain for moral judgments on the antitrust issue. Whereas "sentimentalists" had argued that the trusts should conform to conventional standards of decency and legality, and had urged restrictive and punitive sanctions, Brandeis' solution to the trust problem emphasized instead the expunging of legal and economic conditions that encouraged the growth of trusts. By hitting at the institutional roots of corporate concentration, Brandeis appeared to have adopted a "scientific" method. Yet this appraisal misses the point that Brandeis' animus toward business concentration was itself founded on deeply moral and even personal preferences. His opposition to big business, in other words, had

[29] Quoted in Jacob de Haas, *Louis D. Brandeis: A Biographical Sketch* (Bloch Publ. Co., 1929), p. 44.

more of the qualities of a prejudice than of a conclusion founded upon coherent analysis.

His celebrated fight against the New Haven-Boston & Maine Railroad merger suggests this most clearly. Brandeis began his fight with the conclusion that Morgan's New Haven Railroad empire should not be allowed to absorb New England's transportation system—first, because he distrusted concentrated power and perhaps Morgan as well (a reasonable prejudice), and second, because it offended his sensibilities to see New York replace Boston as the center of control over major New England enterprises, removing them from the reach and presumed inspiration of the region's venerable laws and ideals. ("One by one" Boston's railroad empire passed out of "her dominion," he wrote in *Other People's Money,* until even "her control of the railroads of Massachusetts [was] limited to [32 miles of minor lines].") During the course of the controversy, Brandeis advanced arguments about the evils of "monopoly" (a relatively weak argument to apply to a regulated public utility), about the inefficiency of "banker-management" (generally cogent perhaps but essentially irrelevant here because the management of the railroads was merely changing bankers, not undergoing any structural change), and about the insolvency of the New Haven (a point devastating to the integrity of the New Haven's management but not to the general argument for railroad consolidations). But these contentions came secondarily, both in time and consideration, to Brandeis' prideful conclusion about the undesirability of Morgan's "invasion" of New England.

Other People's Money and How the Bankers Use It, prepared in 1913 in the form of a series of magazine articles, bears the full mark of Brandeis' dual qualities. It is seductively impressive in its presentation of data; it exposes the arrogance of much of American business leadership; and it raises questions about the legitimacy of corporate capitalism to which no one has yet found fully satisfactory answers. Nevertheless, the book has a journalistic simplicity that raises questions about how seriously to regard the whole effort.

III

Brandeis began writing the series under the title "Breaking the Money Trust" while Congress was debating the Federal Reserve Act and beginning deliberations on the Clayton and Federal Trade

Commission Acts. It was not so much to influence legislation, however, that he undertook the task (he had rather more direct channels of influence as one of President Wilson's advisors) as to help Norman Hapgood launch his editorship of the new *Harper's Weekly*. Brandeis might have had an audience of 100,000 or more had he published instead in *Collier's* or *Saturday Evening Post*. But his friend Hapgood had just been forced out of *Collier's*, "superficially on the Wilson-Roosevelt issue," wrote Hapgood, "but more fundamentally, as I see it, on the issue of business control of editorial policy."[30] Advertisers' pressures by 1912 had indeed begun turning the tide against political muckraking, and Hapgood apparently seemed "too controversial" to remain *Collier's* chief editor. This was just the sort of thing Brandeis had come to regard with acute outrage.

Brandeis had himself made most of the business arrangements for the purchase of the *Weekly*. Charles R. Crane, a progressive Chicago plumbing magnate, underwrote the entire $450,000 stock issue for the new Harper's Weekly Corporation, taking $100,000 of the securities himself and helping to persuade Julius Rosenwald, Cleveland Dodge, and three other Chicago businessmen to subscribe to $50,000 each; McClure's Publications provided certain plant and promotional facilities. The *Weekly* was supposed to survive on its sales price and on such advertising as sought it out, with the small group of progressive financiers recruited by Brandeis and Crane prepared to underwrite its early years. "The men who own *Harper's Weekly*," Hapgood wrote to E. W. Scripps, soliciting his aid, "do not care to make much money out of it."[31] In addition to helping recruit the financial backing, handling the legal details, and writing the feature articles on the "money trust," Brandeis also paid for free distribution of thousands of copies of the magazine in order to promote interest in it (and in his articles). In turn, Hapgood took care of the arrangements for publishing a modification of the articles in book form; he negotiated with Macmillan, Bobbs Merrill, and finally Frederick A. Stokes who took on the job in January 1914.

Hapgood and Stokes had wanted the book to be called *Every Man's Money and What the Bankers Do with It*, but Brandeis

[30] Hapgood to Cleveland Dodge, Jan. 12, 1914; in Brandeis MSS.
[31] Hapgood to E. W. Scripps, Dec. 11, 1913; to Brandeis, Oct. 31, 1912 and Dec. 3, 1913; and J. Russell Smith to Brandeis, Jan. 6, 1914; all in Brandeis MSS.

himself preferred *Other People's Money,* perhaps noting Adam Smith's use of the phrase in *The Wealth of Nations:*

> The directors of [joint stock] companies, . . . being the managers rather of other people's money than of their own, it cannot well be expected, that they should watch over it with the same anxious vigilance with which partners in a private copartnery frequently watch over their own. . . . Negligence and profusion, therefore, must always prevail, more or less, in the management of the affairs of such a company.[32]

Smith had argued that because of their inherent—one might almost say *moral*—defects, joint stock companies, or corporations, could never survive in competition with private or proprietary companies unless the state accorded them special privileges—and that such privileges should be granted only if a company were indispensable to the public welfare. Smith of course hardly anticipated the day when a society would regard the survival of practically *all* forms of non-state enterprise as conducive to the public welfare, and thus to justify blanket privileges to corporate business; nor did he conceive of the conditions wherein a society would accept such superior financial power as an enterprise achieved through incorporation to be a legitimate instrument of competition. Louis Brandeis' own opposition to modern corporate capitalism owed much to assumptions he shared with Smith. Although he did not condemn corporate enterprise itself, he held to the view that most "large" corporations suffered the inherent defects Smith spoke of and were indeed baneful to the public welfare. He was confident they could never survive except with "artificial" privileges granted them by the state. Moreover, in his analyses of the relative inefficiency of large scale enterprise, he too ruled out financial power as a quality of efficiency and regarded the use of it for competitive purposes as tantamount to an unfair trade practice.

In his attempt to demonstrate the economic inefficiency of corporate consolidations Brandeis contributed the first serious challenge to the principal rationale of the consolidation movement. Whatever some contemporaries had thought of the social consequences, nearly everyone had at least tacitly conceded the economic superiority of consolidated corporate enterprise. Brandeis noted

---

[32] Modern Library edition, p. 700; see also pp. 713, 714.

some obvious flaws: (1) Consolidations often created enterprises too large for the managers to know well what was happening in all of their parts; (2) the bankers who promoted the combinations and usually dominated their management thereafter aggravated the managerial problem by taking on tasks for which they were poorly trained and which, moreover, contained responsibilities that conflicted with their duties as bankers; (3) to the extent that consolidations reduced competition they contributed to economic inefficiency in the definitional sense that interference with the market mechanism necessarily creates imperfect satisfaction of consumer demand; (4) interlocking directorates similarly vitiated open market bargaining among interdependent firms and led to misallocation of resources and maldistribution of income; (5) corporations sometimes used the monopolistic power deriving from consolidations both to suppress new entries into an industry and to tie up any invention or innovation that jeopardized existing capital investments—an economic gain for a particular firm but a greater economic loss for the society; (6) above all, concentration of money resources was not only conducive to discriminatory credit practices but also inflated the cost of money for new capital investments or new business starts, thus distorting the business advantages of the big corporations; generally, constricted competition in the money market tends to constrict potential competition in all sectors, with necessarily deleterious effects upon the normal incentives for cost-cutting efficiencies in the economy.

The inefficiency argument served as an attempt to meet the consolidationists on their own terms. It has many weaknesses. How big is "too big"? Modern technology and managerial techniques since the 1910's clearly provide a degree of efficiency for some giant corporations that no small nineteenth century firm could have hoped to match. Moreover, the stolid provincialism of the small family firm is legend; economic historians have argued that its persistence in key industries in countries like England and France may well account for their relatively slow economic growth in the twentieth century. Many modern industrial processes require productive capacities that represent a high percentage-share of the total market in order to maintain optimal technical efficiency; even if firms in such industries sacrificed some managerial efficiency, their productive economies more than adequately compensate for the managerial diseconomies ostensibly inherent in their size.

Bigness, moreover, must not be equated with monopoly. Brandeis never seems to have considered that in industries characterized by small firms, single firms often enjoy monopolistic power in their local markets, whereas in large-firm industries, any single firm might represent real or potential competition in every market. Nor is there in Brandeis' writings a concession of any virtue in industrial diversification; in chapter VIII, "A Curse of Bigness," for example, he treats as a general prescription the I.C.C.'s specific observation of fact that "a most prolific source of financial disaster and complication to railroads in the past has been the desire and ability of railroad managers to engage in enterprises outside the legitimate operation of their railroads. . . ." He suggests that the tendency of large firms to enter relatively nonrelated fields represents merely banker-management's overweening ambition for power, frequently leading to disastrous consequences for the original operating company. Yet, whatever the blunders of any particular managements (such as those in the railroad industry), diversification not only can serve the economic function of hedging against losses in any single line but may also provide the general economy with the only practical source of competition for firms in established industries that require extensive marketing mechanisms and heavy capital outlays. Moreover, what Brandeis regarded as loss, at least to the stockholders of a parent corporation, can often represent an aggregate social gain, if, say, in the absorption by a strong railroad of the debts of weaker lines brought into a consolidation, the absorbed lines can be kept in service despite their inherent weaknesses.

Even the privileged access to capital that giant corporations typically enjoy has redeeming qualities that Brandeis does not hint at. For Brandeis, the preferred credit status of the giant corporations represents an uneconomic trade advantage that typically derives from demand-denying factors such as the interlocking directorates of the creditor and debtor companies and the abnormally high profit opportunities that accrue to monopoly power; it is an advantage, moreover, that tends to conceal operating inefficiencies and subdues cost-cutting incentives. Yet the achievement of privileged access to credit may also represent a kind of business efficiency (as distinct from technical or managerial efficiency) that enables the giant corporation to experiment with innovation more readily than less endowed firms, to engage in long-range research projects, to recruit the best available talent, and generally to invest in ventures for which the returns may not materialize for many years. Above all, the greater stability inherent in the large corporation, due to its generally diversified and integrated structure as well as to its credit resources, enables it to absorb losses more readily without dissolution. Such a capability can represent a real social saving not only in the salvaging of at least the founding energies and capital of the enterprise but in the conservation of the energies and fortunes of its labor force and of dependent enterprises in its locality.

IV

Brandeis never relented in his effort to establish his argument about the relative inefficiency of large scale business enterprise. He believed the Great Crash and the Depression confirmed his views since, along with many economists, he was able to argue that price rigidities due to monopolistic market power had distorted capital distribution and consumer income and had been the principal cause of the crippling overproduction-underconsumption impasse. To this analysis Brandeis added the point that large-scale business inefficiencies were at the bottom of the rigid and inflated industrial prices. Convinced of the enduring cogency of his position, Brandeis had *Other People's Money* reissued in 1933 in a cheap paperbound volume. (Hapgood again wrote an introduction.) Meanwhile, through innumerable protegés and disciples, most notably Felix Frankfurter, Brandeis exerted considerable influence on New Deal policies. In fact, for New Dealers like Rex Tugwell, who envisioned a rationalized cooperative commonwealth built upon consolidated and coordinated productive units throughout the country, Brandeis came to represent the principal obstructionist, a "doctrinaire parading as an instrumentalist," according to Tugwell, and the one man most "responsible for the failure of the New Deal."[33] Among intellectuals who generally shared Tugwell's vision and who remain disappointed with the small modifications of the American business system that the New Deal achieved, Brandeis continues to stand in rather poor favor.

Brandeis refused to believe that it was entirely too late even in the 'thirties to create a more rational economic system based on competition. What he observed during the Depression and in

---

[33] Quoted in Arthur M. Schlesinger, Jr., *The Politics of Upheaval* (Houghton Mifflin, 1960), p. 391.

the workings of the NRA only strengthened his convictions about the inefficiency of the corporate giants. Even the doubts of two leading economists whom he hired to write an introduction for the reissue of *Business: A Profession* (also published originally in 1914) failed to dissuade him. Both men, James C. Bonbright and Gardiner Means, had established reputations as critics of certain features of corporate capitalism, and Means especially— in *The Modern Corporation and Private Property*, co-authored with Adolf A. Berle, Jr. in 1932—had forecast a frightening future with a handful of corporations controlling practically all the industrial assets in the country. In 1932, and again in 1935, Means urged Brandeis to reconsider his thesis on bigness, showing him statistics that indicated the consistently higher profitability of corporations with assets over $50 million as compared with corporations with assets under $50,000. Brandeis' answer to this was, as always, that the profitability of the larger corporations derived from attributes other than efficiency; specifically (turning Means' own pioneering thesis of administered prices against him), the ability of the big corporations to control prices through the exercise of monopolistic power. Moreover, even when some big corporations showed efficiencies, they appropriated the full benefits for themselves, leaving none of the surplus to society generally.[34]

Brandeis' argument about attributes "other than efficiency" is something of a question-begger. And yet its kernel of validity rests on the point that there is no way of testing the relative efficiency of small- and large-scale enterprises in an economy that presents both side by side. In a mixed economy, big corporations inevitably have clear advantages over small businesses in marketing, research, credit privileges, legal resources, the recruitment of managerial and sales talent, control of patents, technology, and even political influence. Yet it is not clear whether the aggregate efficiency of an entirely small-business economy would not be greater than that of either the mixed economy we have now or an entirely big-business economy. For in an entirely small-firm economy, small business would enjoy the benefits of the general pool of entrepreneurial talents, as in the nineteenth century; one could reasonably assume that no half-dozen firms would receive

[34] Louis Wehle to Means, Aug. 16, 1932; Wehle to Brandeis, Aug. 16, 1932; Means to Brandeis, Feb. 15, 1935. James Bonbright ultimately wrote the Foreword, though it was rewritten (and his disagreements with Brandeis on several points somewhat muted) by Brandeis' nephew, Louis Wehle.

some 20 to 25 per cent of government funds for research, or employ 20 per cent of all non-institutional and privately-employed technical and scientific personnel, as they do today; and conceivably, legal, credit, patent, and marketing advantages would tend to be rather more evenly distributed.

The key to Brandeis' thought, however, lies not in the efficiency argument but in his belief that the trusts represent a threat to democratic processes and, above all, to the institutional bases of individual liberty and sound national character. He took for granted that economic power was readily translated into political power, and that concentrated economic power necessarily jeopardized the political safeguards of liberal society. But more importantly, Brandeis saw corporate consolidation threatening to expunge the very features of the open, innovative society that had been America's most distinctive mark in the context of western civilization. For most of the country's history, social policy had favored the new and the emancipating. In conflicts of privilege between an innovative force and the vested rights of established interests, American law and practice in the nineteenth century had consistently favored the former: young industries received tariff protection even at the expense of old economic interests; land and internal improvements policies created new market and production centers often to the disadvantage of the interests clustered about the old; there is even evidence to argue that the courts more often than not broke the force of contracts which appeared to stand in the way of desired change. Brandeis was disinclined to consider the aggregate social loss inherent in the relative instability of small business enterprises, even if he could have been persuaded that such loss exceeded the ostensible efficiency costs of more stable, large-scale enterprises. In brief, Brandeis feared most deeply that the centralized power implicit in corporate consolidation must inevitably force the transfer of privilege in American social policy from the innovative and enterprising to the vested interests.

The basis of Brandeis' objections to big business, then, was moral and political rather than economic, even though he insisted the economic argument reinforced his case. ". . . Even more important than efficiency," he says in the book, "are industrial and political liberty." Business concentration must be dissolved whatever the supposed costs in efficiency.

The rise of "the money trust"—the ascendancy of investment banking and the phenomenon of interlocking corporate directorates

—highlighted for Brandeis the nexus between the moral and economic issues. Corporate concentration fostered the money trust by making it impossible for small, independent banks to finance an important share of the nation's business. The big investment bankers thus gained an especially strong position in the credit market; and—as Brandeis put it—they "use their strong position to make an excessive charge." In order to strike at concentration Brandeis argued that prohibitions against interlocking directorates, proposed in the 1913 legislation for the banking industry, be extended to all corporations. "Interlocking directorates . . . [offend] laws human and divine. . . . [They are] undemocratic, . . . [They substitute] the pull of privilege for the push of manhood." In essence, Brandeis was arguing for a return to proprietary capitalism in a corporate form, wherein a particular firm would be run by men undivided in their loyalties, energies, and attention even though they might not in fact be *owners;* although the corporate form of business organization and the recruitment of capital would remain, so too would all the moral incentives of proprietary capitalism.

Brandeis' complaint about the investment bankers' using their "strong position" to demand high prices would seem remarkably anomalous if we took literally his advocacy of free market competition. But one suspects that the marketplace never really operated legitimately for Brandeis without the limitations implied in the notion of a "just price." Convention dictated for him that certain practices were proper and improper, moral and immoral, regardless of whether they formally broke any economic rules. In this respect, the investment banker was the greatest transgressor. Not only did he engage in activities that transcended his "legitimate" province, but "even where his business is properly conducted," Brandeis wrote, even "within his legitimate province," the investment banker presented a "menace [to] the public welfare." For the investment banker held the most vital business resources in his tight fists, and made his profits and built his power upon the strength of money that did not belong to him.

Here we arrive at the charge Brandeis features in this book. Brandeis seems to have resented most of all the fact that investment bankers achieved their wealth and power without risking anything of their own—they used *other people's money.* For an economist, the use of the phrase in this context must appear spurious. For, essentially the banker's claim to the use of deposits for his own profit does not differ critically from, say, a shoemaker's claim to the use of the machines he leases. But Brandeis' argument eludes the economist again because it rests on his contention that there is a proper and an improper use of money left with (rented to?) the banks of deposit. The *proper* function of banks, he asserts, is to serve as "depositaries . . . of the business man's quick capital;" instead, he writes, as though astounded by the force of his accusation, "these institutions . . . have become . . . large purchasers of bonds and stocks"—that is, they have been enticed by the investment bankers who control them into serving as sources of equity capital and loans for the expansion of corporate capitalism. "The power and the growth of power of our financial oligarchs comes from wielding the savings and quick capital of others," Brandeis writes. "The fetters of the people are forged with the people's own gold." And so: "We must put an end to this improper wealth getting, as well as to improper combination."

V

When Brandeis began *Other People's Money,* he wrote to his brother, Alfred (Sept. 2, 1913): "Have had a rather quiet time . . . trying to write some articles on the Money Trust for Harpers. There will be some crys [*sic*] of 'Holy Murder' if the Legislation I propose ever gets past [*sic*]—but less than that will do little good." The provisions of the Federal Reserve Act, the Federal Trade Commission, and the Clayton Antitrust Act, of course, fell far short of what Brandeis prescribed—and they did "little good" in reducing the degree of concentration of control in the American economy. Nothing in the Federal Reserve Act can be described as seriously designed to provide small or new business with the credit needed to survive in competition with the credit power of the big corporations. Congress, moreover, put off enforcing the prohibition against interlocking bank directorates for two years, and then every two years for eight years thereafter it repeated the postponement until the matter was finally dropped. Equivocations on the same subject in the Clayton Act permitted the courts to sanction interlocking directorates of nonbanking corporations. Furthermore, while in its "determination" to strike down holding companies Congress forbade corporations to buy the *securities* of other corporations (if such purchases tended "to substantially lessen competition"), it permitted corporations to purchase the *physical assets* of other corporations, apparently without regard to the effect upon competition. Congress also established a commission to ascertain and terminate certain forms of what Brandeis had called "the competition that kills," even if it should mean sanctioning price and market-quota agreements by trade associations designed to keep even the least efficient firm in business. Finally, Wilson's Justice Department inaugurated the practice of "consent decrees" that has had a variety of effects, not the least of which has been a tendency to give official sanction to the advantageous trade position of an offending firm, even while ostensibly condemning the business practices that had given the firm its trade advantages. In sum, Wilson's New Freedom failed to touch upon, much less alter, the principal sources of concentrated power in the economy, and one can find Brandeis in 1915, 1925, and 1935 advising the necessity of curbing economic concentration as if nothing at all had happened. Practically speaking, nothing had.

Today, most accounts of business developments in the United States seem to begin with the assumption that corporate power and the problem of antitrust policy are no longer serious concerns—that they represent bygone reform issues of the progressive and populist eras, or at best, issues that died with the collapse of the holding company boom of the 1920's and the rectifying legislation of the New Deal. Those who would revive the issue are usually met with a "don't-tell-me-you're-still-playing-that-old-tune" air. John Kenneth Galbraith about sums it up in his *American Capitalism* (1951 edition) :[35] "The [unsophisticated] liberal contemplates with alarm the great corporations which cannot be accommodated to his faith, and, with the conservative, he shares the belief that, whatever the quality of current performance, it is certain not to last. Yet, in the present we survive." Thomas C. Cochran adopts essentially the same position in *The American Business System*,[36] noting the failure of the Brandeisian efforts to restore a condition of market-determined prices and resource allocation, and conceding that the failure has meant both economic inefficiencies and probably higher prices, Cochran concludes nevertheless that "the situation [has] seemed, on the whole, to satisfy the public."

The antitrust efforts of the Brandeisians, so it would seem from the reigning attitude expressed in most recent treatment of the subject, were not only simple-minded and futile, but also

[35] (Houghton Mifflin, 1952), p. 8.
[36] (Harper Torchbooks, 1957), p. 58.

xl   INTRODUCTION TO THE TORCHBOOK EDITION

unnecessary.[37] In a careful and frequently cited analysis of investigations into economic concentration in the United States during the 1901–1947 period, Maurice Adelman argues: "The extent of concentration shows no tendency to grow and may possibly be declining. Any tendency either way, if it does exist, must be at the pace of a glacial drift."[38] Small businesses, moreover, have been growing in number at a rate that exceeds the population growth. And although nepotism remains a deplorably conspicuous feature of managerial recruitment in many of our top corporations, some evidence suggests that corporate capitalism has improved social mobility. Using such findings, many historians, political scientists, and economists in the past 15 years or so have enjoyed deriding "the Populist-Progressive nightmare . . . expressed in the Pujo Committee's inquiry, in Brandeis' *Other People's Money,* in Wilson's speeches," and elsewhere.[39]

This is not to say that the findings indicate a decentralized, vertically mobile economy that features high levels of innovation and efficiency in the mature industries, and vigorous competition in the most crucial sectors. Adelman himself stresses that although concentration may not have increased since 1901, "the American economy is highly concentrated." The point seems to be, rather, that things are not getting noticeably worse, and in some respects may even be getting a bit better. A. A. Berle, Jr., who, with Gardiner Means in 1932, startled the country with the belated "revelation" about the separation of ownership and control in the American economy, more recently has been telling us that we ought not to be alarmed by the fact that a small group of corporate managements—which he aptly describes as "an automatic self-perpetuating oligarchy" having no enforceable legal responsibility to anyone at all—controls two-thirds of the non-farm economy.

[37] See e.g., G. Warren Nutter, *The Extent of Enterprise Monopoly in the United States, 1899–1939* (Univ. of Chicago Press, 1951); Donald Dewey, *Monopoly in Economics and Law* (Rand McNally, 1959); M. A. Adelman, "The Measurement of Industrial Concentration," *Review of Economics and Statistics,* XXXIII (Nov. 1951); Edward S. Mason, *Economic Concentration and the Monopoly Problem* (Harvard Univ. Press, 1957), esp. chs. 1, 2, 5; John Lintner and J. Keith Butters, "The Effect of Mergers on Industrial Concentration," *Review of Economics and Statistics,* XXXII (1950); Ralph L. Nelson, *Concentration in the Manufacturing Industries of the United States, a Midcentury Report* (Yale Univ. Press, 1963).
[38] "The Measurement of Industrial Concentration," *The Review of Economics and Statistics,* XXXIII (1951), 269–296. See also "Four Comments on 'The Measurement . . .'," *Ibid.,* XXXIV (May 1952), 156–178.
[39] Quoting Richard Hofstadter, "What Happened to the Antitrust Movement?" in E. F. Cheit, ed., *The Business Establishment* (Wiley, 1964), p. 134.

Civilization, he tells us, has always rested primarily on the good will of small groups of crucially-placed men anyway, and he sees signs that the oligarchy he describes has come to be more enlightened and morally sensitive than in the old days.[40] Andrew Hacker concurs with Berle that no one has ever been able to explain "by what right the corporation is entitled to power at all" since it is responsible to no one and is governed by non-public objectives. Yet Hacker can see no acceptable alternative to the autocracy implicit in a corporation-dominated economy, and indeed he expresses his satisfaction that "thus far, corporate America has escaped open attack because the new technology is not yet at the point where its victims outnumber its beneficiaries."[41]

Before we join the modern critics in writing off Brandeis as a false prophet, it might be well to examine the points *conceded* by analysts such as Berle and Hacker. How *does* one justify for a professedly liberal society an economic system that formally belies the moral sanctions of responsible power and legitimate order? Like many others in the progressive era, Brandeis was responding to the discovery that rewards under the new capitalist order were incommensurate with intelligence, talent, hard work, risk-taking, daring, or manliness—in other words, all the important elements of the American capitalist rationale. This troubled Brandeis as it has unaccountably ceased to trouble most modern observers. If we reject Brandeis' objections as "moralistic"—that is, if we condemn as anachronistic his insistence upon the old entrepreneurial ethic in contrast to the practices of corporate capitalism—it behooves us to propose a modern substitute for that ethic. The best that is presently offered—and it is truly the best—is that our economic system "works" (that is, it produces commodity surpluses and has enabled us to win two world wars), that "the public is satisfied," that the beneficiaries of the system still outnumber "its victims," and that whatever the illogic of the whole thing, "in the present we survive." It would seem that we are back with the assumptions of John Moody that national power and affluence need no further justification.

Berle, who is at least troubled enough to discuss the issue, assures us that as "inevitably" as they became giants the big corpora-

---

[40] Berle arrives at this remarkable conclusion in his *The 20th Century Capitalist Revolution* (Harcourt, Brace, 1954), and in *Power Without Property* (Harcourt, Brace, 1959), as well as in numerous articles, notably, "Economic Power and the Free Society," in Andrew Hacker, ed., *The Corporation Take-Over* (Doubleday Anchor, 1965).

[41] *The Corporation Take-Over*, p. 13.

xlii INTRODUCTION TO THE TORCHBOOK EDITION

tions which dominate our economy will eventually "find some claim of legitimacy." For, "legitimacy, responsibility, and accountability," he says, "are essential to any power system if it is to endure." What Berle has not explained—and remarkably few people have even tried—is how corporate capitalism has managed to endure almost three-quarters of a century *without* an intellectually respectable claim to legitimacy.[42]

Perhaps what also needs explaining is why, in midcentury, so many observers have chosen to emphasize the apparent abatement of the trend toward concentration that John Moody and Louis Brandeis called to the attention of their contemporaries 60 years ago. If concentration has not increased, neither has it declined, and considering the level of concentration at the base point of the calculations, one would expect that such a fact should not give rise to so much apparent satisfaction. Conceivably, we should be even more concerned today than Brandeis and his fellows were then. For, in the interim the methods of coordinating business policies—including market-sharing, price-fixing, output quotas, patent restrictions, private licensing, and the like (that is, methods of establishing high levels of monopolistic power over specific markets)—have achieved a degree of perfection undreamed of by Judge Gary and his convivial colleagues in the benighted days of the Gary Dinners. The concentration statistics, moreover, tell us primarily about the intra-industrial shares of particular firms, but very little so far about inter-industrial influence by individual giants through a variety of relationships with subsidiaries, affiliates, and simply "friendly" corporate peers. DuPont's relationship with General Motors, its patent arrangements with Standard Oil, General Electric's ties to the electrical utilities, and the relationship of all the giants to the major financial institutions, represent a degree of economy-wide control by a small segment of the "automatic self-perpetuating oligarchy" that has all but escaped close analysis. Nor have economists done much in the way of calculating the incidental impact of the *conglomerate* consolidations on such

---

[42] The usual "legitimation" of the present system of private corporate management focuses on the system's "economic performance"—specifically, the high rate of economic growth and the unparalleled standard of living that Americans enjoy. This is, of course, an elaboration on the argument that "it works," and does not really fit the category of a justification within principles relevant to a liberal society. But it is also argued that the growth of Federal regulatory powers subjects even the giant corporations to satisfactory public restraints, and that these restraints make private corporations "responsible to" public policy. To the extent that the latter is true, governmental regulation offers some formal legitimation to corporate policies.

economic problems as innovation, new entry, the sensitivity of capital flows to market pressures, or the constriction of alternative economic policies for the nation at large. The conglomerates, indeed, present a dimension of "bigness" that Brandeis hardly touched on; for, even where a company's market share in one particular industry may be small, the inter-industrial *scope* of the company may give it advantages in that particular industry that its market share alone would not seem to indicate.[43]

Over and above all these (conceivably) disconcerting matters is the fact that in the last 40 years business leaders have acquired remarkable skills in "public relations" techniques to go with the financial resources they have had for "taste making," the shaping of opinion, and political manipulation. This may indeed be of especial importance for the one major problem that has so far borne little scrutiny: how corporate capitalism has managed for 60 years to employ the presumably outmoded moral rationale of proprietary capitalism to justify its own institutions and practices. Indeed, the rationale has served so well that even today there is only limited acknowledgment that the American business economy since the 1890's has borne but a grossly distorted resemblance to a free market economy. This has to be explained before we come to complacent conclusions about the "inevitability" of corporate giantism or about the general public satisfaction with corporate capitalism's performance.

When our economists and historians, and the professional surveys they rely on, report that a substantial majority of the American people respond favorably to big business, how much of the apparent satisfaction is due to the very power of the corporate oligarchies in question? Are we to understand that the public has been satisfied with the performance of corporate capitalism because the results have satisfied real needs, or is it that "public relations" efforts have persuaded the public that its needs could be satisfied in no other way or no more completely? How do we know how efficiently our corporate enterprises are functioning if entry and innovation are seriously constricted in most of the important sectors of the economy? How do we know how responsive to public demand corporate decisions are if the mass communications media, which are susceptible to great commercial pressure, have

[43] For an introduction to the subject, see Corwin Edwards, "Conglomerate Big Business as a Source of Power," in *Business Concentration and Price Policy,* A Conference of Universities-National Bureau Committee for Economic Research (Princeton Univ. Press, 1955), pp. 331–359.

generally advised "the public" that there are no palatable alternatives? When we consider how the Supreme Court, by emasculating antitrust legislation (that surely must represent some measure of public sentiment), appeared to have shut off at an early date many real alternatives to an economy dominated by big corporate enterprise, is it meaningful at all to speak of "the public's satisfaction," the "inevitability" of it all, and the historical absence of feasible alternatives? Moreover, can anyone show, without being tautological, that corporate America has escaped open attack because its beneficiaries still outnumber its victims? Have the victims, however numerous, ever been in a position to launch an open attack? When we consider, after all, that political discussion in the last half-century has dwelt inordinately upon "the threat from the left," and particularly how emphasis upon a not unreal international revolutionary movement has successfully linked the fear of the left with anxieties about national security, how can we be confident that serious proposals on the social and political problem created by big corporate enterprise have ever received a fair hearing?

Brandeis' *Other People's Money* is of course primarily valuable for what it tells us about the antitrust movement in the progressive era. It shows its age in the various weaknesses of its argument. But even for our time, now a half century later, only a willful reluctance to test fundamentals can obscure its refreshing pertinence.

CHAPTER I

OUR FINANCIAL OLIGARCHY

PRESIDENT WILSON, when Governor, declared in 1911:

"The great monopoly in this country is the money monopoly. So long as that exists, our old variety and freedom and individual energy of development are out of the question. A great industrial nation is controlled by its system of credit. Our system of credit is concentrated. The growth of the nation, therefore, and all our activities are in the hands of a few men, who, even if their actions be honest and intended for the public interest, are necessarily concentrated upon the great undertakings in which their own money is involved and who, necessarily, by every reason of their own limitations, chill and check and destroy genuine economic freedom. This is the greatest question of all; and to this, statesmen must address themselves with an earnest determination to serve the long future and the true liberties of men."

The Pujo Committee—appointed in 1912—found:

"Far more dangerous than all that has happened to us in the past in the way of elimination of competition in industry is the control of credit through the domination of these groups over our banks and industries." . . .

"Whether under a different currency system the re-

1

sources in our banks would be greater or less is comparatively immaterial if they continue to be controlled by a small group." . . .

"It is impossible that there should be competition with all the facilities for raising money or selling large issues of bonds in the hands of these few bankers and their partners and allies, who together dominate the financial policies of most of the existing systems. . . . The acts of this inner group, as here described, have nevertheless been more destructive of competition than anything accomplished by the trusts, for they strike at the very vitals of potential competition in every industry that is under their protection, a condition which if permitted to continue, will render impossible all attempts to restore normal competitive conditions in the industrial world. . . .

"If the arteries of credit now clogged well-nigh to choking by the obstructions created through the control of these groups are opened so that they may be permitted freely to play their important part in the financial system, competition in large enterprises will become possible and business can be conducted on its merits instead of being subject to the tribute and the good will of this handful of self-constituted trustees of the national prosperity."

The promise of New Freedom was joyously proclaimed in 1913.

The facts which the Pujo Investigating Committee and its able Counsel, Mr. Samuel Untermyer, have laid before the country, show clearly the means by which a few men control the business of America. The report proposes measures which promise some relief. Additional remedies will be proposed. Congress will soon be called upon to act.

How shall the emancipation be wrought? On what

lines shall we proceed? The facts, when fully understood, will teach us.

THE DOMINANT ELEMENT

The dominant element in our financial oligarchy is the investment banker. Associated banks, trust companies and life insurance companies are his tools. Controlled railroads, public service and industrial corporations are his subjects. Though properly but middlemen, these bankers bestride as masters America's business world, so that practically no large enterprise can be undertaken successfully without their participation or approval. These bankers are, of course, able men possessed of large fortunes; but the most potent factor in their control of business is not the possession of extraordinary ability or huge wealth. The key to their power is Combination—concentration intensive and comprehensive—advancing on three distinct lines:

First: There is the obvious consolidation of banks and trust companies; the less obvious affiliations—through stockholdings, voting trusts and interlocking directorates—of banking institutions which are not legally connected; and the joint transactions, gentlemen's agreements, and "banking ethics" which eliminate competition among the investment bankers.

Second: There is the consolidation of railroads into huge systems, the large combinations of public service corporations and the formation of industrial trusts, which, by making businesses so "big" that local, independent banking concerns cannot alone supply the necessary funds, has created dependence upon the associated New York bankers.

But combination, however intensive, along these lines only, could not have produced the Money Trust

—another and more potent factor of combination was added.

Third: Investment bankers, like J. P. Morgan & Co., dealers in bonds, stocks and notes, encroached upon the functions of the three other classes of corporations with which their business brought them into contact. They became the directing power in railroads, public service and industrial companies through which our great business operations are conducted—the makers of bonds and stocks. They became the directing power in the life insurance companies, and other corporate reservoirs of the people's savings—the buyers of bonds and stocks. They became the directing power also in banks and trust companies—the depositaries of the quick capital of the country—the life blood of business, with which they and others carried on their operations. Thus four distinct functions, each essential to business, and each exercised, originally, by a distinct set of men, became united in the investment banker. It is to this union of business functions that the existence of the Money Trust is mainly due.*

The development of our financial oligarchy followed, in this respect, lines with which the history of political despotism has familiarized us:—usurpation, proceeding by gradual encroachment rather than by violent acts; subtle and often long-concealed concentration of distinct functions, which are beneficent when separately administered, and dangerous only when combined in the same persons. It was by processes such as these that Cæsar Augustus became master of Rome. The makers of our own Constitution had in mind like

---

* Obviously only a few of the investment bankers exercise this great power; but many others perform important functions in the system, as hereinafter described.

dangers to our political liberty when they provided so carefully for the separation of governmental powers.

THE PROPER SPHERE OF THE INVESTMENT BANKER

The original function of the investment banker was that of dealer in bonds, stocks and notes; buying mainly at wholesale from corporations, municipalities, states and governments which need money, and selling to those seeking investments. The banker performs, in this respect, the function of a merchant; and the function is a very useful one. Large business enterprises are conducted generally by corporations. The permanent capital of corporations is represented by bonds and stocks. The bonds and stocks of the more important corporations are owned, in large part, by small investors, who do not participate in the management of the company. Corporations require the aid of a banker-middleman, for they lack generally the reputation and clientele essential to selling their own bonds and stocks direct to the investor. Investors in corporate securities, also, require the services of a banker-middleman. The number of securities upon the market is very large. Only a part of these securities is listed on the New York Stock Exchange; but its listings alone comprise about sixteen hundred different issues aggregating about $26,500,000,000, and each year new listings are made averaging about two hundred and thirty-three to an amount of $1,500,000,000. For a small investor to make an intelligent selection from these many corporate securities—indeed, to pass an intelligent judgment upon a single one—is ordinarily impossible. He lacks the ability, the facilities, the training and the time essential to a proper investigation. Unless his purchase is to be little better than a gamble, he needs the advice of an expert, who, combining special knowledge with judgment, has the facilities and incentive to make a thorough investigation. This dependence, both of corporations and of investors, upon the banker has grown in recent years, since women and others who do not participate in the management, have become the owners of so large a part of the stocks and bonds of our great corporations. Over half of the stockholders of the American Sugar Refining Company and nearly half of the stockholders of the Pennsylvania Railroad and of the New York, New Haven & Hartford Railroad are women.

Good-will—the possession by a dealer of numerous and valuable regular customers—is always an important element in merchandising. But in the business of selling bonds and stocks, it is of exceptional value, for the very reason that the small investor relies so largely upon the banker's judgment. This confidential relation of the banker to customers and the knowledge of the customers' private affairs acquired incidentally—is often a determining factor in the marketing of securities. With the advent of Big Business such good-will possessed by the older banking houses, preëminently J. P. Morgan & Co. and their Philadelphia House called Drexel & Co., by Lee, Higginson & Co. and Kidder, Peabody, & Co. of Boston, and by Kuhn, Loeb & Co. of New York, became of enhanced importance. The volume of new security issues was greatly increased by huge railroad consolidations, the development of the holding companies, and particularly by the formation of industrial trusts. The rapidly accumulating savings of our people sought investment. The field of operations for the dealer in securities was thus much enlarged. And, as the securities were new and untried, the services of the investment banker were in great demand, and his powers and profits increased accordingly.

CONTROLLING THE SECURITY MAKERS

But this enlargement of their legitimate field of operations did not satisfy investment bankers. They were not content merely to deal in securities. They desired to manufacture them also. They became promoters, or allied themselves with promoters. Thus it was that J. P. Morgan & Company formed the Steel Trust, the Harvester Trust and the Shipping Trust. And, adding the duties of undertaker to those of midwife, the investment bankers became, in times of corporate disaster, members of security-holders' "Protective Committees"; then they participated as "Reorganization Managers" in the reincarnation of the unsuccessful corporations and ultimately became directors. It was in this way that the Morgan associates acquired their hold upon the Southern Railway, the Northern Pacific, the Reading, the Erie, the Père Marquette, the Chicago and Great Western, and the Cincinnati, Hamilton & Dayton. Often they insured the continuance of such control by the device of the voting trust; but even where no voting trust was created, a secure hold was acquired upon reorganization. It was in this way also that Kuhn, Loeb & Co. became potent in the Union Pacific and in the Baltimore & Ohio.

But the banker's participation in the management of corporations was not limited to cases of promotion or reorganization. An urgent or extensive need of new money was considered a sufficient reason for the banker's entering a board of directors. Often without even such excuse the investment banker has se-

---

[1] Brandeis was in error about the organization of International Harvester. Letters in the George W. Perkins papers and the McCormick family collections prove that the initiative for this came from

cured a place upon the Board of Directors, through
his powerful influence or the control of his customers'
proxies. Such seems to have been the fatal entrance
of Mr. Morgan into the management of the then prosperous New York, New Haven & Hartford Railroad,
in 1892. When once a banker has entered the Board—
whatever may have been the occasion—his grip proves
tenacious and his influence usually supreme; for he
controls the supply of new money.

The investment banker is naturally on the lookout
for good bargains in bonds and stocks. Like other
merchants he wants to buy his merchandise cheap. But
when he becomes director of a corporation, he oc-
cupies a position which prevents the transaction by
which he acquires its corporate securities from being
properly called a bargain. Can there be real bargaining where the same man is on both sides of a trade?
The investment banker, through his controlling influence on the Board of Directors, decides that the
corporation shall issue and sell the securities, decides
the price at which it shall sell them, and decides that
it shall sell the securities to himself. The fact that
there are other directors besides the banker on the
Board does not, in practice, prevent this being the
result. The banker, who holds the purse-strings, becomes usually the dominant spirit. Through voting-
trusteeships, exclusive financial agencies, membership
on executive or finance committees, or by mere directorships, J. P. Morgan & Co., and their associates, held
such financial power in at least thirty-two transportation systems, public utility corporations and industrial
companies—companies with an aggregate capitalization
of $17,273,000,000. Mainly for corporations so con-
trolled, J. P. Morgan & Co. procured the public marketing in ten years of security issues aggregating $1,950,-

---

the McCormick and Deering families, who owned the two largest
companies in the agricultural implements industry, and not from promotional ambitions of investment bankers. J. P. Morgan & Company,

000,000. This huge sum does not include any issues marketed privately, nor any issues, however, marketed, of intra-state corporations. Kuhn, Loeb & Co. and a few other investment bankers exercise similar control over many other corporations.

CONTROLLING SECURITY BUYERS

Such control of railroads, public service and industrial corporations assures to the investment bankers an ample supply of securities at attractive prices; and merchandise well bought is half sold. But these bond and stock merchants are not disposed to take even a slight risk as to their ability to market their goods. They saw that if they could control the security-buyers, as well as the security-makers, investment banking would, indeed, be "a happy hunting ground"; and they have made it so.

The numerous small investors cannot, in the strict sense, be controlled; but their dependence upon the banker insures their being duly influenced. A large part, however, of all bonds issued and of many stocks are bought by the prominent corporate investors; and most prominent among these are the life insurance companies, the trust companies, and the banks. The purchase of a security by these institutions not only relieves the banker of the merchandise, but recommends it strongly to the small investor, who believes that these institutions are wisely managed. These controlled corporate investors are not only large customers, but may be particularly accommodating ones. Individual investors are moody. They buy only when they want to do so. They are sometimes inconveniently reluctant. Corporate investors, if controlled, may be made to buy when the bankers need a market. It

---

however, did make the best of its opportunities once negotiations began. The promotional factor in the organization of United States Steel is a more difficult problem: Alfred Chandler and others have pointed

was natural that the investment bankers proceeded to get control of the great life insurance companies, as well as of the trust companies and the banks.

The field thus occupied is uncommonly rich. The life insurance companies are our leading institutions for savings. Their huge surplus and reserves, augmented daily, are always clamoring for investment. No panic or money shortage stops the inflow of new money from the perennial stream of premiums on existing policies and interest on existing investments. The three great companies—the New York Life, the Mutual of New York, and the Equitable—would have over $55,000,000 of *new* money to invest annually, even if they did not issue a single new policy. In 1904—just before the Armstrong investigation—these three companies had together $1,247,331,738.18 of assets. They had issued in that year $1,025,671,126 of new policies. The New York legislature placed in 1906 certain restrictions upon their growth; so that their new business since has averaged $547,384,212, or only fifty-three per cent. of what it was in 1904. But the aggregate assets of these companies increased in the last eight years to $1,817,052,260.36. At the time of the Armstrong investigation the average age of these three companies was fifty-six years. *The growth of assets in the last eight years was about half as large as the total growth in the preceding fifty-six years.* These three companies must invest annually about $70,000,000 of new money; and besides, many old investments expire or are changed and the proceeds must be reinvested. A large part of all life insurance surplus and reserves are invested in bonds. The aggregate bond investments of these three companies on January 1, 1913, was $1,019,153,268.93.

It was natural that the investment bankers should

out that, like International Harvester, its organization derived from fears within the industry about over-capacity and price-cutting rather than from the initiative of investment bankers. On the other hand, the

seek to control these never-failing reservoirs of capital. George W. Perkins was Vice-President of the New York Life, the largest of the companies. While remaining such he was made a partner in J. P. Morgan & Co., and in the four years preceding the Armstrong investigation, his firm sold the New York Life $38,-804,918.51 in securities. The New York Life is a mutual company, supposed to be controlled by its policy holders. But as the Pujo Committee finds "the so-called control of life insurance companies by policy-holders through mutualization is a farce" and "its only result is to keep in office a self-constituted, self-perpetuating management."

The Equitable Life Assurance Society is a stock company and is controlled by $100,000 of stock. The dividend on this stock is limited by law to seven per cent.; but in 1910 Mr. Morgan paid about $3,000,000 for $51,000, par value of this stock, or $5,882.35 a share. The dividend return on the stock investment is less than one-eighth of one per cent.; but the assets controlled amount now to over $500,000,000. And certain of these assets had an especial value for investment bankers;—namely, the large holdings of stock in banks and trust companies.

The Armstrong investigation disclosed the extent of financial power exerted through the insurance company holdings of bank and trust company stock. The Committee recommended legislation compelling the insurance companies to dispose of the stock within five years. A law to that effect was enacted, but the time was later extended. The companies then disposed of a part of their bank and trust company stocks; but, as the insurance companies were controlled by the investment bankers, these gentlemen sold the bank and trust company stocks to themselves.

---

fact that J. P. Morgan was already a dominant figure in several constituent companies absorbed by the combination lends substance to Brandeis' accusation.

Referring to such purchases from the Mutual Life, as well as from the Equitable, the Pujo Committee found:

"Here, then, were stocks of five important trust companies and one of our largest national banks in New York City that had been held by these two life insurance companies. Within five years all of these stocks, so far as distributed by the insurance companies, have found their way into the hands of the men who virtually controlled or were identified with the management of the insurance companies or of their close allies and associates, to that extent thus further entrenching them."

The banks and trust companies are depositaries, in the main, not of the people's savings, but of the business man's quick capital. Yet, since the investment banker acquired control of banks and trust companies, these institutions also have become, like the life companies, large purchasers of bonds and stocks. Many of our national banks have invested in this manner a large part of all their resources, including capital, surplus and deposits. The bond investments of some banks exceed by far the aggregate of their capital and surplus, and nearly equal their loanable deposits.

CONTROLLING OTHER PEOPLE'S QUICK CAPITAL

The goose that lays golden eggs has been considered a most valuable possession. But even more profitable is the privilege of taking the golden eggs laid by somebody else's goose. The investment bankers and their associates now enjoy that privilege. They control the people through the people's own money. If the bankers' power were commensurate only with their wealth, they would have relatively little influence

on American business. Vast fortunes like those of
the Astors are no doubt regrettable. They are inconsistent with democracy. They are unsocial. And
they seem peculiarly unjust when they represent largely
unearned increment. But the wealth of the Astors
does not endanger political or industrial liberty. It
is insignificant in amount as compared with the aggregate wealth of America, or even of New York City.
It lacks significance largely because its owners have
only the income from their own wealth. The Astor
wealth is static. The wealth of the Morgan associates
is dynamic. The power and the growth of power of
our financial oligarchs comes from wielding the savings
and quick capital of others. In two of the three great
life insurance companies the influence of J. P. Morgan
& Co. and their associates is exerted without any individual investment by them whatsoever. Even in
the Equitable, where Mr. Morgan bought an actual
majority of all the outstanding stock, his investment
amounts to little more than one-half of one per cent.
of the assets of the company. The fetters which bind
the people are forged from the people's own gold.

But the reservoir of other people's money, from
which the investment bankers now draw their greatest
power, is not the life insurance companies, but the
banks and the trust companies. Bank deposits represent the really quick capital of the nation. They are
the life blood of businesses. Their effective force is
much greater than that of an equal amount of wealth
permanently invested. The 34 banks and trust companies, which the Pujo Committee declared to be directly controlled by the Morgan associates, held $1,-
983,000,000 in deposits. Control of these institutions
means the ability to lend a large part of these funds,
directly and indirectly, to themselves; and what is

often even more important, the power to prevent the funds being lent to any rival interests. These huge deposits can, in the discretion of those in control, be used to meet the temporary needs of their subject corporations. When bonds and stocks are issued to finance permanently these corporations, the bank deposits can, in large part, be loaned by the investment bankers in control to themselves and their associates; so that securities bought may be carried by them, until sold to investors. Or these bank deposits may be loaned to allied bankers, or jobbers in securities, or to speculators, to enable them to carry the bonds or stocks. Easy money tends to make securities rise in the market. Tight money nearly always makes them fall. The control by the leading investment bankers over the banks and trust companies is so great, that they can often determine, for a time, the market for money by lending or refusing to lend on the Stock Exchange. In this way, among others, they have power to affect the general trend of prices in bonds and stocks. Their power over a particular security is even greater. Its sale on the market may depend upon whether the security is favored or discriminated against when offered to the banks and trust companies, as collateral for loans.

Furthermore, it is the investment banker's access to other people's money in controlled banks and trust companies which alone enables any individual banking concern to take so large part of the annual output of bonds and stocks. The banker's own capital, however large, would soon be exhausted. And even the loanable funds of the banks would often be exhausted, but for the large deposits made in those banks by the life insurance, railroad, public service, and industrial corporations which the bankers also control. On

December 31, 1912, the three leading life insurance companies had deposits in banks and trust companies aggregating $13,839,189.08. As the Pujo Committee finds:

"The men who through their control over the funds of our railroads and industrial companies are able to direct where such funds shall be kept and thus to create these great reservoirs of the people's money, are the ones who are in position to tap those reservoirs for the ventures in which they are interested and to prevent their being tapped for purposes of which they do not approve. The latter is quite as important a factor as the former. It is the controlling consideration in its effect on competition in the railroad and industrial world."

HAVING YOUR CAKE AND EATING IT TOO

But the power of the investment banker over other people's money is often more direct and effective than that exerted through controlled banks and trust companies. J. P. Morgan & Co. achieve the supposedly impossible feat of having their cake and eating it too. They buy the bonds and stocks of controlled railroads and industrial concerns, and pay the purchase price; and still do not part with their money. This is accomplished by the simple device of becoming the bank of deposit of the controlled corporations, instead of having the company deposit in some merely controlled bank in whose operation others have at least some share. When J. P. Morgan & Co. buy an issue of securities the purchase money, instead of being paid over to the corporation, is retained by the banker for the corporation, to be drawn upon only as the funds are needed by the corporation. And as the securities are issued in large blocks, and the money raised is often not all spent until long thereafter, the aggregate of the balances remaining in the bankers' hands are huge. Thus J. P. Morgan & Co. (including their Philadelphia house, called Drexel & Co.) held on November 1, 1912, deposits aggregating $162,491,819.65.

POWER AND PELF

The operations of so comprehensive a system of concentration necessarily developed in the bankers overweening power. And the bankers' power grows by what it feeds on. Power begets wealth; and added wealth opens ever new opportunities for the acquisition of wealth and power. The operations of these bankers are so vast and numerous that even a very reasonable compensation for the service performed by the bankers, would, in the aggregate, produce for them incomes so large as to result in huge accumulations of capital. But the compensation taken by the bankers as commissions or profits is often far from reasonable. Occupying, as they so frequently do, the inconsistent position of being at the same time seller and buyer, the standard for so-called compensation actually applied, is not the "Rule of reason", but "All the traffic will bear." And this is true even where there is no sinister motive. The weakness of human nature prevents men from being good judges of their own deservings.

The syndicate formed by J. P. Morgan & Co. to underwrite the United States Steel Corporation took for its services securities which netted $62,500,000 in cash. Of this huge sum J. P. Morgan & Co. received, as syndicate managers, $12,500,000 in addition to the share which they were entitled to receive as syndicate members. This sum of $62,500,000 was only a part of the fees paid for the service of monopolizing the steel industry. In addition to the commissions taken specifically for organizing the United States Steel Corporation, large sums were paid for organizing the several companies of which it is composed. For instance, the National Tube Company was capitalized at $80,-000,000 of stock; $40,000,000 of which was common stock. Half of this $40,000,000 was taken by J. P. Morgan & Co. and their associates for promotion services; and the $20,000,000 stock so taken became later exchangeable for $25,000,000 of Steel Common. Commissioner of Corporations Herbert Knox Smith found that:

"More than $150,000,000 of the stock of the Steel Corporation was issued directly or indirectly (through exchange) for mere promotion or underwriting services. In other words, nearly one-seventh of the total capital stock of the Steel Corporation appears to have been issued directly or indirectly to promoters' services."

The so-called fees and commissions taken by the bankers and associates upon the organization of the trusts have been exceptionally large. But even after the trusts are successfully launched the exactions of the bankers are often extortionate. The syndicate which underwrote, in 1901, the Steel Corporation's preferred stock conversion plan, advanced only $20,-000,000 in cash and received an underwriting commission of $6,800,000.

The exaction of huge commissions is not confined to trust and other industrial concerns. The Interborough Railway is a most prosperous corporation. It earned last year nearly 21 per cent. on its capital stock, and secured from New York City, in connection with the subway extension, a very favorable contract. But when it financed its $170,000,000 bond issue it was agreed that J. P. Morgan & Co. should receive three per cent., that is, $5,100,000, for merely forming this syndicate. More recently, the New York, New Haven & Hartford Railroad agreed to pay J. P. Morgan & Co. a commission of $1,680,000; that is, 2½ per cent., to form a syndicate to underwrite an issue at par of $67,000,000 20-year 6 per cent. convertible debentures. That means: The bankers bound themselves to take at 97½ any of these six per cent. convertible bonds which stockholders might be unwilling to buy at 100. When the contract was made the New Haven's then outstanding six per cent. convertible bonds were selling at 114. And the new issue, as soon as announced, was in such demand that the public offered and was for months willing to buy at 106 bonds which the Company were to pay J. P. Morgan & Co. $1,680,000 to be willing to take at par.

WHY THE BANKS BECAME INVESTMENT BANKERS

These large profits from promotions, underwritings and security purchases led to a revolutionary change in the conduct of our leading banking institutions. It was obvious that control by the investment bankers of the deposits in banks and trust companies was an essential element in their securing these huge profits. And the bank officers naturally asked, "Why then should not the banks and trust companies share in so profitable a field? Why should not they themselves become investment bankers too, with all the new functions incident to 'Big Business'?" To do so would involve a departure from the legitimate sphere of the banking business, which is the making of temporary loans to business concerns. But the temptation was irresistible. The invasion of the investment banker into the banks' field of operation was followed by a counter invasion by the banks into the realm of the investment banker. Most prominent among the banks were the National City and the First National of New York. But theirs was not a hostile invasion. The contending forces met as allies, joined forces to control the business of the country, and to "divide the spoils." The alliance was cemented by voting trusts, by interlocking directorates and by joint ownerships. There resulted the fullest "cooperation"; and ever more railroads, public service corporations, and industrial concerns were brought into complete subjection.

CHAPTER II

HOW THE COMBINERS COMBINE

AMONG the allies, two New York banks—the National City and the First National—stand preëminent. They constitute, with the Morgan firm, the inner group of the Money Trust. Each of the two banks, like J. P. Morgan & Co., has huge resources. Each of the two banks, like the firm of J. P. Morgan & Co., has been dominated by a genius in combination. In the National City it is James Stillman; in the First National, George F. Baker. Each of these gentlemen was formerly President, and is now Chairman of the Board of Directors. The resources of the National City Bank (including its Siamese-twin security company) are about $300,000,000; those of the First National Bank (including its Siamese-twin security company) are about $200,000,000. The resources of the Morgan firm have not been disclosed. But it appears that they have available for their operations, also, huge deposits from their subjects; deposits reported as $162,500,000.

The private fortunes of the chief actors in the combination have not been ascertained. But sporadic evidence indicates how great are the possibilities of accumulation when one has the use of "other people's money." Mr. Morgan's wealth became proverbial. Of Mr. Stillman's many investments, only one was specifically referred to, as he was in Europe during the investigation, and did not testify. But that one is significant. His 47,498 shares in the National City Bank are worth about $18,000,000. Mr. Jacob H. Schiff [2] aptly described this as "a very nice investment."

Of Mr. Baker's investments we know more, as he testified on many subjects. His 20,000 shares in the First National Bank are worth at least $20,000,000. His stocks in six other New York banks and trust companies are together worth about $3,000,000. The scale of his investment in railroads may be inferred from his former holdings in the Central Railroad of New Jersey. He was its largest stockholder—so large that with a few friends he held a majority of the $27,-436,800 par value of outstanding stock, which the Reading bought at $160 a share. He is a director in 28 other railroad companies; and presumably a stockholder in, at least, as many. The full extent of his fortune was not inquired into, for that was not an issue in the investigation. But it is not surprising that Mr. Baker saw little need of new laws. When asked:

"You think everything is all right as it is in this world, do you not?"

He answered:

"Pretty nearly."

---

[2] Jacob Henry Schiff, 1847–1920, head of Kuhn, Loeb & Company from 1885 virtually until his death.

RAMIFICATIONS OF POWER

But wealth expressed in figures gives a wholly inadequate picture of the allies' power. Their wealth is dynamic. It is wielded by geniuses in combination. It finds its proper expression in means of control. To comprehend the power of the allies we must try to visualize the ramifications through which the forces operate.

Mr. Baker is a director in 22 corporations having, with their many subsidiaries, aggregate resources or capitalization of $7,272,000,000. But the direct and visible power of the First National Bank, which Mr. Baker dominates, extends further. The Pujo report shows that its directors (including Mr. Baker's son) are directors in at least 27 other corporations with resources of $4,270,000,000. That is, the First National is represented in 49 corporations, with aggregate resources or capitalization of $11,542,000,000.

It may help to an appreciation of the allies power to name a few of the more prominent corporations in which, for instance, Mr. Baker's influence is exerted—visibly and directly—as voting trustee, executive committee man or simple director.

1. *Banks, Trust, and Life Insurance Companies*: First National Bank of New York; National Bank of Commerce; Farmers' Loan and Trust Company; Mutual Life Insurance Company.

2. *Railroad Companies*: New York Central Lines; New Haven, Reading, Erie, Lackawanna, Lehigh Valley, Southern, Northern Pacific, Chicago, Burlington & Quincy.

3. *Public Service Corporations*: American Telegraph & Telephone Company, Adams Express Company.

4. *Industrial Corporations*: United States Steel Corporation, Pullman Company.

Mr. Stillman is a director in only 7 corporations, with aggregate assets of $2,476,000,000; but the directors in the National City Bank, which he dominates, are directors in at least 41 other corporations which, with their subsidiaries, have an aggregate capitalization or resources of $10,564,000,000. The members of the firm of J. P. Morgan & Co., the acknowledged leader of the allied forces, hold 72 directorships in 47 of the largest corporations of the country.

The Pujo Committee finds that the members of J. P. Morgan & Co. and the directors of their controlled trust companies and of the First National and the National City Bank together hold:

"One hundred and eighteen directorships in 34 banks and trust companies having total resources of $2,679,-000,000 and total deposits of $1,983,000,000.

"Thirty directorships in 10 insurance companies having total assets of $2,293,000,000.

"One hundred and five directorships in 32 transportation systems having a total capitalization of $11,-784,000,000 and a total mileage (excluding express companies and steamship lines) of 150,200.

"Sixty-three directorships in 24 producing and trading corporations having a total capitalization of $3,-339,000,000.

"Twenty-five directorships in 12 public-utility corporations having a total capitalization of $2,150,-000,000.

"In all, 341 directorships in 112 corporations having aggregate resources or capitalization of $22,245,-000,000"

TWENTY-TWO BILLION DOLLARS

"Twenty-two billion dollars is a large sum—so large that we have difficulty in grasping its significance. The mind realizes size only through comparisons. With what can we compare twenty-two billions of dollars? Twenty-two billions of dollars is more than three times the assessed value of all the property, real and personal, in all New England. It is nearly three times the assessed value of all the real estate in the City of New York. It is more than twice the assessed value of all the property in the thirteen Southern states. It is more than the assessed value of all the property in the twenty-two states, north and south, lying west of the Mississippi River.

But the huge sum of twenty-two billion dollars is not large enough to include all the corporations to which the "influence" of the three allies, directly and visibly, extends, for

First: There are 56 other corporations (not included in the Pujo schedule) each with capital or resources of over $5,000,000, and aggregating nearly $1,350,000,-000, in which the Morgan allies are represented according to the directories of directors.

Second: The Pujo schedule does not include any corporation with resources of less than $5,000,000. But these financial giants have shown their humility by becoming directors in many such. For instance, members of J. P. Morgan & Co., and directors in the National City Bank and the First National Bank are also directors in 158 such corporations. Available publications disclose the capitalization of only 38 of these, but those 38 aggregate $78,669,375.

Third: The Pujo schedule includes only the corporations in which the Morgan associates actually appear by name as directors. It does not include those in which they are represented by dummies, or otherwise. For instance, the Morgan influence certainly extends to the Kansas City Terminal Railway Company, for which they have marketed since 1910 (in connection with others) four issues aggregating $41,-761,000. But no member of J. P. Morgan & Co., of the National City Bank, or of the First National Bank appears on the Kansas City Terminal directorate.

Fourth: The Pujo schedule does not include all the subsidiaries of the corporations scheduled. For instance, the capitalization of the New Haven System is given as $385,000,000. That sum represents the bond and stock capital of the New Haven *Railroad*. But the New Haven *System* comprises many controlled corporations whose capitalization is only to a slight extent included directly or indirectly in the New Haven Railroad balance sheet. The New Haven, like most large corporations, is a holding company also; and a holding company may control subsidiaries, while owning but a small part of the latters' outstanding securities. Only the small part so held will be represented in the holding company's balance sheet. Thus, while the New Haven Railroad's capitalization is only $385,000,000—and that sum only appears in the Pujo schedule—the capitalization of the New Haven System, as shown by a chart submitted to the Committee, is over twice as great; namely, $849,000,000.

It is clear, therefore, that the $22,000,000,000, referred to by the Pujo Committee, understates the extent of concentration effected by the inner group of the Money Trust.

CEMENTING THE TRIPLE ALLIANCE

Care was taken by these builders of imperial power that their structure should be enduring. It has been buttressed on every side by joint ownerships and mutual stockholdings, as well as by close personal relationships; for directorships are ephemeral and may end with a new election. Mr. Morgan and his partners acquired one-sixth of the stock of the First National Bank, and made a $6,000,000 investment in the stock of the National City Bank. Then J. P. Morgan & Co., the National City, and the First National (or their dominant officers—Mr. Stillman and Mr. Baker) acquired together, by stock purchases and voting trusts, control of the National Bank of Commerce, with its $190,000,000 of resources; of the Chase National, with $125,000,000; of the Guaranty Trust Company, with $232,000,000; of the Bankers' Trust Company, with $205,000,000; and of a number of smaller, but important, financial institutions. They became joint voting trustees in great railroad systems; and finally (as if the allies were united into a single concern) loyal and efficient service in the banks—like that rendered by Mr. Davison and Mr. Lamont in the First National—was rewarded by promotion to membership in the firm of J. P. Morgan & Co.

THE PROVINCIAL ALLIES

Thus equipped and bound together, J. P. Morgan & Co., the National City and the First National easily dominated America's financial center, New York; for certain other important bankers, to be hereafter mentioned, were held in restraint by "gentlemen's" agreements. The three allies dominated Philadelphia too; for the firm of Drexel & Co. is J. P. Morgan & Co. under another name. But there are two other important money centers in America, Boston and Chicago.

In Boston there are two large international banking houses—Lee, Higginson & Co., and Kidder, Peabody & Co.—both long established and rich, and each possessing an extensive, wealthy clientele of eager investors in bonds and stocks. Since 1907 each of these firms has purchased or underwritten (principally in conjunction with other bankers) about 100 different security issues of the greater interstate corporations, the issues of each banker amounting in the aggregate to over $1,000,000,000. Concentration of banking capital has proceeded even further in Boston than in New York. By successive consolidations the number of national banks has been reduced from 58 in 1898 to 19 in 1913. There are in Boston now also 23 trust companies.

The National Shawmut Bank, the First National Bank of Boston and the Old Colony Trust Co., which these two Boston banking houses and their associates control, alone have aggregate resources of $288,-386,294, constituting about one-half of the banking resources of the city. These great banking institutions, which are themselves the result of many consolidations, and the 21 other banks and trust companies, in which their directors are also directors, hold together 90 per cent. of the total banking resources of Boston. And linked to them by interlocking directorates are 9 other banks and trust companies whose aggregate resources are about 2 1/2 per cent. of Boston's total. Thus of 42 banking institutions, 33, with aggregate resources of $560,516,239, holding about

92 1/2 per cent. of the aggregate banking resources of
Boston, are interlocked. But even the remaining 9
banks and trust companies, which together hold but
7 1/2 per cent. of Boston banking resources, are not
all independent of one another. Three are linked together; so that there appear to be only six banks in
all Boston that are free from interlocking directorate
relations. They together represent but 5 per cent. of
Boston's banking resources. And it may well be
doubted whether all of even those 6 are entirely free
from affiliation with the other groups.

Boston's banking concentration is not limited to the
legal confines of the city. Around Boston proper are
over thirty suburbs, which with it form what is pop-
ularly known as "Greater Boston." These suburban
municipalities, and also other important cities like
Worcester and Springfield, are, in many respects, within Boston's "sphere of influence." Boston's inner
banking group has interlocked, not only 33 of the 42
banks of Boston proper, as above shown, but has
linked with them, by interlocking directorships, at least
42 other banks and trust companies in 35 other municipalities.

Once Lee, Higginson & Co. and Kidder, Peabody &
Co. were active competitors. They are so still in some
small, or purely local matters; but both are devoted co-
operators with the Morgan associates in larger and interstate transactions; and the alliance with these great
Boston banking houses has been cemented by mutual
stockholdings and co-directorships. Financial concentration seems to have found its highest expression in
Boston.

Somewhat similar relations exist between the triple
alliance and Chicago's great financial institutions—its
First National Bank, the Illinois Trust and Savings

Bank, and the Continental & Commercial National Bank—which together control resources of $561,-000,000. And similar relations would doubtless be found to exist with the leading bankers of the other important financial centers of America, as to which the Pujo Committee was prevented by lack of time from making investigation.

THE AUXILIARIES

Such are the primary, such the secondary powers which comprise the Money Trust; but these are supplemented by forces of magnitude.

"Radiating from these principal groups," says the Pujo Committee, "and closely affiliated with them are smaller but important banking houses, such as Kissel, Kinnicut & Co., White, Weld & Co., and Harvey Fisk & Sons, who receive large and lucrative patronage from the dominating groups, and are used by the latter as jobbers or distributors of securities, the issuing of which they control, but which for reasons of their own they prefer not to have issued or distributed under their own names. Lee, Higginson & Co., besides being partners with the inner group, are also frequently utilized in this service because of their facilities as distributors of securities."

For instance, J. P. Morgan & Co. as fiscal agents of the New Haven Railroad had the right to market its securities and that of its subsidiaries. Among the numerous New Haven subsidiaries, is the New York, Westchester and Boston—the road which cost $1,500,000 a mile to build, and which earned a *deficit* last year of nearly $1,500,000, besides failing to earn any return upon the New Haven's own stock and bond investment of $8,241,951. When the New Haven concluded to market $17,200,000 of these bonds, J. P. Morgan & Co., "for reasons of their own," "preferred not to have these bonds issued or distributed under their own name." The Morgan firm took the bonds at 92 1/2 net; and the bonds were marketed by Kissel, Kinnicut & Co. and others at 96 1/4.

THE SATELLITES

The alliance is still further supplemented as the Pujo Committee shows:

"Beyond these inner groups and sub-groups are banks and bankers throughout the country who co-operate with them in underwriting or guaranteeing the sale of securities offered to the public, and who also act as distributors of such securities. It was impossible to learn the identity of these corporations, owing to the unwillingness of the members of the inner group to disclose the names of their underwriters, but sufficient appears to justify the statement that there are at least hundreds of them and that they extend into many of the cities throughout this and foreign countries.

"The patronage thus proceeding from the inner group and its sub-groups is of great value to these banks and bankers, who are thus tied by self-interest to the great issuing houses and may be regarded as a part of this vast financial organization. Such patronage yields no inconsiderable part of the income of these banks and bankers and without much risk on account of the facilities of the principal groups for placing issues of securities through their domination of great banks and trust companies and their other domestic affiliations and their foreign connections. The underwriting commissions on issues made by this inner group are usually easily earned and do not ordinarily involve the underwriters in the purchase of the underwritten securities. Their interest in the transaction is generally adjusted unless they choose to purchase part of the securities, by the payment to them of a commission. There are, however, occasions on which this is not the case. The underwriters are then required to take the securities. Bankers and brokers are so anxious to be permitted to participate in these transactions under the lead of the inner group that as a rule they join when invited to do so, regardless of their approval of the particular business, lest by refusing they should thereafter cease to be invited."

In other words, an invitation from these royal bankers is interpreted as a command. As a result, these great bankers frequently get huge commissions without themselves distributing any of the bonds, or ever having taken any actual risk.

"In the case of the New York subway financing of $170,000,000 of bonds by Messrs. Morgan & Co. and their associates, Mr. Davison [as the Pujo Committee reports] estimated that there were from 100 to 125 such underwriters who were apparently glad to agree that Messrs. Morgan & Co., the First National Bank, and the National City Bank should receive 3 per cent., —equal to $5,100,000—for forming this syndicate, thus relieving themselves from all liability whilst the underwriters assumed the risk of what the bonds would realize and of being required to take their share of the unsold portion."

THE PROTECTION OF PSEUDO-ETHICS

The organization of the Money Trust is intensive, the combination comprehensive; but one other element

[3] Henry P. Davison, Vice President of the First National Bank of New York, and after 1908 a partner in J. P. Morgan & Company.

was recognized as necessary to render it stable, and to make its dynamic force irresistible. Despotism, be it financial or political, is vulnerable, unless it is believed to rest upon a moral sanction. The longing for freedom is ineradicable. It will express itself in protest against servitude and inaction unless the striving for freedom be made to seem immoral. Long ago monarchs invented, as a preservative of absolutism, the fiction of "The divine right of kings." Bankers, imitating royalty, invented recently that precious rule of so-called "Ethics," by which it is declared unprofessional to come to the financial relief of any corporation which is already the prey of another "reputable" banker.

"The possibility of competition between these banking houses in the purchase of securities," says the Pujo Committee, "is further removed by the understanding between them and others, that one will not seek, by offering better terms, to take away from another, a customer which it has theretofore served, and by corollary of this, namely, that where given bankers have once satisfactorily united in bringing out an issue of a corporation, they shall also join in bringing out any subsequent issue of the same corporations. This is described as a principle of banking ethics."

The "Ethical" basis of the rule must be that the interests of the combined bankers are superior to the interests of the rest of the community. Their attitude reminds one of the "spheres of influence" with ample "hinterlands" by which rapacious nations are adjusting differences. Important banking concerns, too ambitious to be willing to take a subordinate position in the alliance, and too powerful to be suppressed, are accorded a financial "sphere of influence" upon the understanding that the rule of banking ethics will be faithfully observed. Most prominent among such lesser potentates

are Kuhn, Loeb & Co., of New York, an international
banking house of great wealth, with large clientele
and connections. They are accorded an important
"sphere of influence" in American railroading, including among other systems the Baltimore & Ohio,
the Union Pacific and the Southern Pacific. They and
the Morgan group have with few exceptions preëmpted
the banking business of the important railroads of the
country. But even Kuhn, Loeb & Co. are not wholly
independent. The Pujo Committee reports that they
are "qualified allies of the inner group"; and through
their "close relations with the National City Bank and
the National Bank of Commerce and other financial
institutions" have "many interests in common with the
Morgan associates, conducting large joint-account
operations with them."

THE EVILS RESULTANT

First: These banker-barons levy, through their excessive exactions, a heavy toll upon the whole community; upon owners of money for leave to invest it;
upon railroads, public service and industrial companies,
for leave to use this money of other people; and,
through these corporations, upon consumers.

"The charge of capital," says the Pujo Committee,
"which of course enters universally into the price of
commodities and of service, is thus in effect determined by agreement amongst those supplying it and
not under the check of competition. If there be any
virtue in the principle of competition, certainly any plan
or arrangement which prevents its operation in the
performance of so fundamental a commercial function
as the supplying of capital is peculiarly injurious."

Second: More serious, however, is the effect of the

Money Trust in directly suppressing competition. That suppression enables the monopolist to extort excessive profits; but monopoly increases the burden of the consumer even more in other ways. Monopoly arrests development; and through arresting development, prevents that lessening of the cost of production and of distribution which would otherwise take place.

Can full competition exist among the anthracite coal railroads when the Morgan associates are potent in all of them? And with like conditions prevailing, what competition is to be expected between the Northern Pacific and the Great Northern, the Southern, the Louisville and Nashville, and the Atlantic Coast Line; or between the Westinghouse Manufacturing Company and the General Electric Company? As the Pujo Committee finds:

"Such affiliations tend as a cover and conduit for secret arrangements and understandings in restriction of competition through the agency of the banking house thus situated."

And under existing conditions of combination, relief through other banking houses is precluded.

"It can hardly be expected that the banks, trust companies, and other institutions that are thus seeking participation from this inner group would be likely to engage in business of a character that would be displeasing to the latter or would interfere with their plans or prestige. And so the protection that can be afforded by the members of the inner group constitutes the safest refuge of our great industrial combinations against future competition. The powerful grip of these gentlemen is upon the throttle that controls the wheels of credit, and upon their signal those wheels will turn or stop."

Third: But far more serious even than the suppression of competition is the suppression of industrial liberty, indeed of manhood itself, which this overweening financial power entails. The intimidation which it effects extends far beyond "the banks, trust companies, and other institutions seeking participation from this inner group in their lucrative underwritings"; and far beyond those interested in the great corporations directly dependent upon the inner group. Its blighting and benumbing effect extends as well to the small and seemingly independent business man, to the vast army of professional men and others directly dependent upon "Big Business," and to many another; for

1. Nearly every enterprising business man needs bank credit. The granting of credit involves the exercise of judgment of the bank officials; and however honestly the bank officials may wish to exercise their discretion, experience shows that their judgment is warped by the existence of the all-pervading power of the Money Trust. He who openly opposes the great interests will often be found to lack that quality of "safe and sane"-ness which is the basis of financial credit.

2. Nearly every enterprising business man and a large part of our professional men have something to sell to, or must buy something from, the great corporations to which the control or influence of the money lords extends directly, or from or to affiliated interests. Sometimes it is merchandise; sometimes it is service; sometimes they have nothing either to buy or to sell, but desire political or social advancement. Sometimes they want merely peace. Experience shows that "it is not healthy to buck against a locomotive," and "Business is business."

Here and there you will find a hero,—red-blooded,

and courageous—loving manhood more than wealth, place or security,—who dared to fight for independence and won. Here and there you may find the martyr, who resisted in silence and suffered with resignation. But America, which seeks "the greatest good of the greatest number," cannot be content with conditions that fit only the hero, the marytr or the slave.

CHAPTER III

INTERLOCKING DIRECTORATES

The practice of interlocking directorates is the root of many evils. It offends laws human and divine. Applied to rival corporations, it tends to the suppression of competition and to violation of the Sherman law. Applied to corporations which deal with each other, it tends to disloyalty and to violation of the fundamental law that no man can serve two masters. In either event it tends to inefficiency; for it removes incentive and destroys soundness of judgment. It is undemocratic, for it rejects the platform: "A fair field and no favors," —substituting the pull of privilege for the push of manhood. It is the most potent instrument of the Money Trust. Break the control so exercised by the investment bankers over railroads, public-service and industrial corporations, over banks, life insurance and trust companies, and a long step will have been taken toward attainment of the New Freedom.

The term "Interlocking directorates" is here used in a broad sense as including all intertwined conflicting interests, whatever the form, and by whatever device effected. The objection extends alike to contracts of a corporation whether with one of its directors indidivually, or with a firm of which he is a member, or with another corporation in which he is interested as an officer or director or stockholder. The objection extends likewise to men holding the inconsistent position of director in two potentially competing corporations, even if those corporations do not actually deal with each other.

THE ENDLESS CHAIN

A single example will illustrate the vicious circle of control—the endless chain—through which our financial oligarchy now operates:

J. P. Morgan (or a partner), a director of the New York, New Haven & Hartford Railroad, causes that company to sell to J. P. Morgan & Co. an issue of bonds. J. P. Morgan & Co. borrow the money with which to pay for the bonds from the Guaranty Trust Company, of which Mr. Morgan (or a partner) is a director. J. P. Morgan & Co. sell the bonds to the Penn Mutual Life Insurance Company, of which Mr. Morgan (or a partner) is a director. The New Haven spends the proceeds of the bonds in purchasing steel rails from the United States Steel Corporation, of which Mr. Morgan (or a partner) is a director. The United States Steel Corporation spends the proceeds of the rails in purchasing electrical supplies from the General Electric Company, of which Mr. Morgan (or a partner) is a director. The General Electric sells supplies to the Western Union Telegraph Company, a subsidiary of the American Telephone and Telegraph Company; and in both Mr. Morgan (or a partner) is a director. The Telegraph Company has an exclusive wire contract with the Reading, of which Mr. Morgan (or a partner) is a director. The Reading buys its passenger cars from the Pullman Company, of which Mr. Morgan (or a partner) is a director. The Pullman Company buys (for local use) locomotives from the Baldwin Locomotive Company, of which Mr. Morgan (or a partner) is a director. The Reading, the General Electric, the Steel Corporation and the New Haven, like the Pullman, buy locomotives from the Baldwin Company. The Steel Corporation, the Telephone Company, the New Haven, the Reading, the Pullman and the Baldwin Companies, like the Western Union, buy electrical supplies from the General Electric. The Baldwin, the Pullman, the Reading, the Telephone, the Telegraph and the General Electric companies, like the New Haven, buy steel products from the Steel Corporation. Each and every one of the companies last named markets its securities through J. P. Morgan & Co.; each deposits its funds with J. P. Morgan & Co.; and with these funds of each, the firm enters upon further operations.

This specific illustration is in part suppositious; but it represents truthfully the operation of interlocking directorates. Only it must be multiplied many times and with many permutations to represent fully the extent to which the interests of a few men are intertwined. Instead of taking the New Haven as the railroad starting point in our example, the New York Central, the Santa Fé, the Southern, the Lehigh Valley, the Chicago and Great Western, the Erie or the Père Marqutte might have been selected; instead of the Guaranty Trust Company as the banking reservoir, any one of a dozen other important banks or trust companies; instead of the Penn Mutual as purchaser of the bonds, other insurance companies; instead of the General Electric, its qualified competitor, the Westinghouse Electric and Manufacturing Company. The chain is indeed endless; for each controlled corporation is entwined with many others.

As the *nexus* of "Big Business" the Steel Corporation stands, of course, preëminent. The Stanley Committee showed that the few men who control the Steel Corporation, itself an owner of important railroads, are directors also in twenty-nine other railroad systems, with 126,000 miles of line (more than half the railroad mileage of the United States), and in important steamship companies. Through all these alliances and the huge traffic it controls, the Steel Corporation's influence pervades railroad and steamship companies—not as carriers only—but as the largest customers for steel. And its influence with users of steel extends much further. These same few men are also directors in twelve steel-using street railway systems, including some of the largest in the world. They are directors in forty machinery and similar steel-using manufacturing companies; in many gas, oil and water companies, extensive users of iron products; and in the great wire-using telephone and telegraph companies. The aggregate assets of these different corporations—through which these few men exert their influence over the business of the United States—exceeds sixteen billion dollars.

Obviously, interlocking directorates, and all that term implies, must be effectually prohibited before the freedom of American business can be regained. The prohibition will not be an innovation. It will merely give full legal sanction to the fundamental law of morals and of human nature: that "No man can serve two masters." The surprising fact is that a principle of equity so firmly rooted should have been departed from at all in dealing with corporations. For no rule of law has, in other connections, been more rigorously

⁴ A House Committee headed by Congressman Augustus O. Stanley (D-Ky.) which launched an investigation of the United States Steel

applied, than that which prohibits a trustee from occupying inconsistent positions, from dealing with himself, or from using his fiduciary position for personal profit. And a director of a corporation is as obviously a trustee as persons holding similar positions in an unincorporated association, or in a private trust estate, who are called specifically by that name. The Courts have recognized this fully.

Thus, the Court of Appeals of New York declared in an important case:

"While not technically trustees, for the title of the corporate property was in the corporation itself, they were charged with the duties and subject to the liabilities of trustees. Clothed with the power of controlling the property and managing the affairs of the corporation without let or hindrance, as to third persons, they were its agents; but as to the corporation itself equity holds them liable as trustees. While courts of law generally treat the directors as agents, courts of equity treat them as trustees, and hold them to a strict account for any breach of the trust relation. For all practical purposes they are trustees, when called upon in equity to account for their official conduct."

NULLIFYING THE LAW

But this wholesome rule of business, so clearly laid down, was practically nullified by courts in creating two unfortunate limitations, as concessions doubtless to the supposed needs of commerce.

First: Courts held valid contracts between a corporation and a director, or between two corporations with a common director, where it was shown that in making the contract, the corporation was represented by independent directors and that the vote of the in-

---

Corporation in January 1912. Brandeis worked briefly for it. In 1911, Brandeis had helped write the LaFollette-Stanley Antitrust bill which sought to shift the burden of proving the "unreasonableness" or "rea-

terested director was unnecessary to carry the motion and his presence was not needed to constitute a quorum.

Second: Courts held that even where a common director participated actively in the making of a contract between two corporations, the contract was not absolutely void, but voidable only at the election of the corporation.

The first limitation ignored the rule of law that a beneficiary is entitled to disinterested advice from *all* his trustees, and not merely from some; and that a trustee may violate his trust by inaction as well as by action. It ignored, also, the laws of human nature, in assuming that the influence of a director is confined to the act of voting. Every one knows that the most effective work is done before any vote is taken, subtly, and without provable participation. Every one should know that the denial of minority representation on boards of directors has resulted in the domination of most corporations by one or two men; and in practically banishing all criticism of the dominant power. And even where the board is not so dominated, there is too often that "harmonious cooperation" among directors which secures for each, in his own line, a due share of the corporation's favors.

The second limitation—by which contracts, in the making of which the interested director participates actively, are held *merely voidable* instead of absolutely void—ignores the teachings of experience. To hold such contracts merely voidable has resulted practically in declaring them valid. It is the directors who control corporate action; and there is little reason to expect that any contract, entered into by a board with a fellow director, however unfair, would be subsequently avoided. Appeals from Philip drunk to Philip sober are not of

---

sonableness" of a corporate merger from government to the merging companies, and in addition to permit court findings of violations of the antitrust laws to serve as conclusive evidence in damage suits by

frequent occurrence, nor very fruitful. But here we lack even an appealing party. Directors and the dominant stockholders would, of course, not appeal; and the minority stockholders have rarely the knowledge of facts which is essential to an effective appeal, whether it be made to the directors, to the whole body of stockholders, or to the courts. Besides, the financial burden and the risks incident to any attempt of individual stockholders to interfere with an existing management is ordinarily prohibitive. Proceedings to avoid contracts with directors are, therefore, seldom brought, except after a radical change in the membership of the board. And radical changes in a board's membership are rare. Indeed the Pujo Committee reports:

"None of the witnesses (the leading American bankers testified) was able to name an instance in the history of the country in which the stockholders had succeeded in overthrowing an existing management in any large corporation. Nor does it appear that stockholders have ever even succeeded in so far as to secure the investigation of an existing management of a corporation to ascertain whether it has been well or honestly managed."

Mr. Max Pam proposed in the April, 1913, Harvard Law Review, that the government come to the aid of minority stockholders. He urged that the president of every corporation be required to report annually to the stockholders, and to state and federal officials every contract made by the company in which any director is interested; that the Attorney-General of the United States or the State investigate the same and take proper proceedings to set all such contracts aside and recover any damages suffered; or without disaffirming the contracts to recover from the interested directors the

---

injured interests. The bill never passed; its provisions were never made law.

profits derived therefrom. And to this end also, that State and National Bank Examiners, State Superintendents of Insurance, and the Interstate Commerce Commission be directed to examine the records of every bank, trust company, insurance company, railroad company and every other corporation engaged in interstate commerce. Mr. Pam's views concerning interlocking directorates are entitled to careful study. As counsel prominently identified with the organization of trusts, he had for years full opportunity of weighing the advantages and disadvantages of "Big Business." His conviction that the practice of interlocking directorates is a menace to the public and demands drastic legislation, is significant. And much can be said in support of the specific measure which he proposes. But to be effective, the remedy must be fundamental and comprehensive.

THE ESSENTIALS OF PROTECTION

Protection to minority stockholders demands that corporations be prohibited absolutely from making contracts in which a director has a private interest, and that all such contracts be declared not voidable merely, but absolutely void.

In the case of railroads and public-service corporations (in contradistinction to private industrial companies), such prohibition is demanded, also, in the interest of the general public. For interlocking interests breed inefficiency and disloyalty; and the public pays, in higher rates or in poor service, a large part of the penalty for graft and inefficiency. Indeed, whether rates are adequate or excessive cannot be determined until it is known whether the gross earnings of the corporation are properly expended. For when a company's important contracts are made through directors who are interested on both sides, the common presumption that money spent has been properly spent does not prevail. And this is particularly true in railroading, where the company so often lacks effective competition in its own field.

But the compelling reason for prohibiting interlocking directorates is neither the protection of stockholders, nor the protection of the public from the incidents of inefficiency and graft. Conclusive evidence (if obtainable) that the practice of interlocking directorates benefited all stockkholders and was the most efficient form of organization, would not remove the objections. For even more important than efficiency are industrial and political liberty; and these are imperiled by the Money Trust. *Interlocking directorates must be prohibited, because it is impossible to break the Money Trust without putting an end to the practice in the larger corporations.*

BANKS AS PUBLIC-SERVICE CORPORATIONS

The practice of interlocking directorates is peculiarly objectionable when applied to banks, because of the nature and functions of those institutions. Bank deposits are an important part of our currency system. They are almost as essential a factor in commerce as our railways. Receiving deposits and making loans therefrom should be treated by the law not as a private business, but as one of the public services. And recognizing it to be such, the law already regulates it in many ways. The function of a bank is to receive and to loan money. It has no more right than a common carrier to use its powers specifically to build up or to destroy other businesses. The granting or withholding of a loan should be determined, so far as concerns the borrower, solely by the interest rate and the risk involved; and not by favoritism or other considerations foreign to the banking function. Men may safely be allowed to grant or to deny loans of their *own* money to whomsoever they see fit, whatsoever their motive may be. But bank resources are, in the main, not owned by the stockholders nor by the directors. Nearly three-fourths of the aggregate resources of the thirty-four banking institutions in which the Morgan associates hold a predominant influence are represented by deposits. The dependence of commerce and industry upon bank deposits, as the common reservoir of quick capital is so complete, that deposit banking should be recognized as one of the businesses "affected with a public interest." And the general rule which forbids public-service corporations from making unjust discriminations or giving undue preference should be applied to the operations of such banks.

Senator Owen, Chairman of the Committee on Banking and Currency, said recently:

"My own judgment is that a bank is a public-utility institution and cannot be treated as a private affair, for the simple reason that the public is invited, under the safeguards of the government, to deposit its money with the bank, and the public has a right to have its interests safeguarded through organized authorities. The logic of this is beyond escape. All banks in the United States, public and private, should be treated as public-utility institutions, where they receive public deposits."

The directors and officers of banking institutions must, of course, be entrusted with wide discretion in the granting or denying of loans. But that discretion should be exercised, not only honestly as it affects stockholders, but also impartially as it affects the public. Mere honesty to the stockholders demands that the interests to be considered by the directors be the interests of all the stockholders; not the profit of the part of them who happen to be its directors. But the general welfare demands of the director, as trustee for the public, performance of a stricter duty. The fact that the granting of loans involves a delicate exercise of discretion makes it difficult to determine whether the rule of equality of treatment, which every public-service corporation owes, has been performed. But that difficulty merely emphasizes the importance of making absolute the rule that banks of deposit shall not make any loan nor engage in any transaction in which a director has a private interest. And we should bear this in mind: If privately-owned banks fail in the public duty to afford borrowers equality of opportunity, there will arise a demand for government-owned banks, which will become irresistible.

The statement of Mr. Justice Holmes of the Supreme Court of the United States, in the Oklahoma Bank case, is significant: [5]

"We cannot say that the public interests to which we have adverted, and others, are not sufficient to warrant the State in taking the whole business of banking under its control. On the contrary we are of opinion that it may go on from regulation to prohibition except upon such conditions as it may prescribe."

OFFICIAL PRECEDENTS

Nor would the requirement that banks shall make no loan in which a director has a private interest impose undue hardships or restrictions upon bank directors. It might make a bank director dispose of some

---

[5] "Oklahoma Bank Case" refers to *Noble State Bank v. Haskill* 219 U.S. 104 and 575 (1911). Holmes wrote the decision for a unanimous Court. The decision upheld an Oklahoma law that set up a state fund to guarantee bank deposits. The opinion became an important precedent

of his investments and refrain from making others; but it often happens that the holding of one office precludes a man from holding another, or compels him to dispose of certain financial interests.

A judge is disqualified from sitting in any case in which he has even the smallest financial interest; and most judges, in order to be free to act in any matters arising in their court, proceed, upon taking office, to dispose of all investments which could conceivably bias their judgment in any matter that might come before them. An Interstate Commerce Commissioner is prohibited from owning any bonds or stocks in any corporation subject to the jurisdiction of the Commission. It is a serious criminal offence for any executive officer of the federal government to transact government business with any corporation in the pecuniary profits of which he is directly or indirectly interested.

And the directors of our great banking institutions, as the ultimate judges of bank credit, exercise today a function no less important to the country's welfare than that of the judges of our courts, the interstate commerce commissioners, and departmental heads.

SCOPE OF THE PROHIBITION

In the proposals for legislation on this subject, four important questions are presented:

1. Shall the principle of prohibiting inter-locking directorates in potentially competing corporations be applied to state banking institutions, as well as the national banks?

2. Shall it be applied to all kinds of corporations or only to banking institutions?

3. Shall the principle of prohibiting corporations from entering into transactions in which the manage-

---

for sustaining, under police power, a broad field of social legislation in the states, and for Federal legislation such as the Glass-Steagall Banking Act of 1933.

ment has a private interest be applied to both directors
and officers or be confined in its application to officers
only?

4. Shall the principle be applied so as to prohibit
transactions with another corporation in which one of
its directors is interested merely as a stockholder?

CHAPTER IV

SERVE ONE MASTER ONLY

The Pujo Committee has presented the facts concerning the Money Trust so clearly that the conclusions
appear inevitable. Their diagnosis discloses intense
financial concentration and the means by which it is
effected. Combination,— the intertwining of interests,
—is shown to be the all-pervading vice of the present
system. With a view to freeing industry, the Committee recommends the enactment of twenty-one specific
remedial provisions. Most of these measures are
wisely framed to meet some abuse disclosed by the
evidence; and if all of these were adopted the Pujo
legislation would undoubtedly alleviate present suffering and aid in arresting the disease. But many of the
remedies proposed are "local" ones; and a cure is not
possible, without treatment which is fundamental. Indeed, a major operation is necessary. This the Committee has hesitated to advise; although the fundamental treatment required is simple: "Serve one Master
only."

The evils incident to interlocking directorates are,
of course, fully recognized; but the prohibitions proposed in that respect are restricted to a very narrow
sphere.

First: The Committee recognizes that potentially

competing corporations should not have a common director;—but it restricts this prohibition to directors of
national banks, saying:

"No officer or director of a national bank shall be
an officer or director of any other bank or of any trust
company or other financial or other corporation or institution, whether organized under state or federal law,
that is authorized to receive money on deposit or that is
engaged in the business of loaning money on collateral
or in buying and selling securities except as in this section provided; and no person shall be an officer or director of any national bank who is a private banker or
a member of a firm or partnership of bankers that is
engaged in the business of receiving deposits: Provided,
That such bank, trust company, financial institution,
banker, or firm of bankers is located at or engaged in
business at or in the same city, town, or village as that
in which such national bank is located or engaged in
business: Provided further, That a director of a national bank or a partner of such director may be an
officer or director of not more than one trust company
organized by the laws of the state in which such national bank is engaged in business and doing business
at the same place."

Second: The Committee recognizes that a corporation should not make a contract in which one of the
management has a private interest; but it restricts this
prohibition (1) to national banks, and (2) to the
officers, saying:

"No national bank shall lend or advance money or
credit or purchase or discount any promissory note,
draft, bill of exchange or other evidence of debt bearing the signature or indorsement of any of its officers
or of any partnership of which such officer is a member, directly or indirectly, or of any corporation in

which such officer owns or has a beneficial interest
of upward of ten per centum of the capital stock, or
lend or advance money or credit to, for or on behalf
of any such officer or of any such partnership or corporation, or purchase any security from any such
officer or of or from any partnership or corporation of
which such officer is a member or in which he is
financially interested, as herein specified, or of any
corporation of which any of its officers is an officer at
the time of such transaction."

Prohibitions of intertwining relations so restricted,
however supplemented by other provisions, will not
end financial concentration. The Money Trust snake
will, at most, be scotched, not killed. The prohibition of
a common director in potentially competing corporations should apply to state banks and trust companies,
as well as to national banks; and it should apply to railroad and industrial corporations as fully as to banking
institutions. The prohibition of corporate contracts in
which one of the management has a private interest
should apply to directors, as well as to officers, and
to state banks and trust companies and to other classes
of corporations, as well as to national banks. And,
as will be hereafter shown, such broad legislation is
within the power of Congress.

Let us examine this further:

THE PROHIBITION OF COMMON DIRECTORS IN PO-
TENTIALLY COMPETING CORPORATIONS

1. *National Banks.* The objection to common directors, as applied to banking institutions, is clearly
shown by the Pujo Committee.

"As the first and foremost step in applying a remedy, and also for reasons that seem to us conclusive,

independently of that consideration, we recommend that interlocking directorates in potentially competing financial institutions be abolished and prohibited so far as lies in the power of Congress to bring about that result. . . . When we find, as in a number of instances, the same man a director in half a dozen or more banks and trust companies all located in the same section of the same city, doing the same class of business and with a like set of associates similarly situated, all belonging to the same group and representing the same class of interests, all further pretense of competition is useless. . . . If banks serving the same field are to be permitted to have common directors, genuine competition will be rendered impossible. Besides, this practice gives to such common directors the unfair advantage of knowing the affairs of borrowers in various banks, and thus affords endless opportunities for oppression."

This recommendation is in accordance with the legislation or practice of other countries, the Bank of England, the Bank of France, the National Bank of Belgium, and the leading banks of Scotland all exclude from their boards persons who are directors in other banks. By law, in Russia no person is allowed to be on the board of management of more than one bank.

The Committee's recommendation is also in harmony with laws enacted by the Commonwealth of Massachusetts more than a generation ago designed to curb financial concentration through the savings banks. Of the great wealth of Massachusetts a large part is represented by deposits in savings banks. These deposits are distributed among 194 different banks, located in 131 different cities and towns. These 194 banks are separate and distinct; not only in form, but in fact. In order that the banks may not be controlled by a few financiers, the Massachusetts law provides that no executive officer or trustee (director) of any savings bank can hold any office in any other savings bank. That statute was passed in 1876. A few years ago it was supplemented by providing that none of the executive officers of a savings bank could hold a similar office in any national bank. Massachusetts attempted thus to curb the power of the individual financier; and no disadvantages are discernible. When that Act was passed the aggregate deposits in its savings banks were $243,-340,642; the number of deposit accounts 739,289; the average deposit to each person of the population $144. On November 1, 1912, the aggregate deposits were $838,635,097.85; the number of deposit accounts 2,-200,917; the average deposit to each account $381.04. Massachusetts has shown that curbing the power of the few, at least in this respect, is entirely consistent with efficiency and with the prosperity of the whole people.

2. *State Banks and Trust Companies.* The reason for prohibiting common directors in banking institutions applies equally to national banks and to state banks including those trust companies which are essentially banks. In New York City there are 37 trust companies of which only 15 are members of the clearing house; but those 15 had on November 2, 1912, aggregate resources of $827,875,653. Indeed the Bankers' Trust Company with resources of $205,000,000, and the Guaranty Trust Company, with resources of $232,000,000, are among the most useful tools of the Money Trust. No bank in the country has larger deposits than the latter; and only one bank larger deposits than the former. If common directorships were permitted in state banks or such trust companies, the charters of leading national banks would doubtless soon

be surrendered; and the institutions would elude federal control by re-incorporating under state laws.

The Pujo Committee has failed to apply the prohibition of common directorships in potentially competing banking institutions rigorously even to national
banks. It permits the same man to be a director in
one national bank and one trust company doing business in the same place. The proposed concession opens
the door to grave dangers. In the first place the provision would permit the interlocking of any national
bank not with one trust company only, but with as
many trust companies as the bank has directors. For
while under the Pujo bill no one can be a national bank
director who is director in more than one such trust
company, there is nothing to prevent each of the directors of a bank from becoming a director in a different
trust company. The National Bank of Commerce of
New York has a board of 38 directors. There are 37
trust companies in the City of New York. Thirty-
seven of the 38 directors might each become a director
of a different New York trust company: and thus 37
trust companies would be interlocked with the National
Bank of Commerce, unless the other recommendation
of the Pujo Committee limiting the number of directors
to 13 were also adopted.

But even if the bill were amended so as to limit the
possible interlocking of a bank to a single trust company, the wisdom of the concession would still be
doubtful. It is true, as the Pujo Committee states, that
"the business that may be transacted by" a trust company is of "a different character" from that properly
transacted by a national bank. But the business actually conducted by a trust company is, at least in the
East, quite similar; and the two classes of banking
institutions have these vital elements in common: each

is a bank of deposit, and each makes loans from its deposits. A private banker may also transact some business of a character different from that properly conducted by a bank; but by the terms of the Committee's bill a private banker engaged in the business of receiving deposits would be prevented from being a director of a national bank; and the reasons underlying that prohibition apply equally to trust companies and to private bankers.

3. *Other Corporations.* The interlocking of banking institutions is only one of the factors which have developed the Money Trust. The interlocking of other corporations has been an equally important element. And the prohibition of interlocking directorates should be extended to potentially competing corporations whatever the class; to life insurance companies, railroads and industrial companies, as well as banking institutions. The Pujo Committee has shown that Mr. George F. Baker is a common director in the six railroads which haul 80 per cent. of all anthracite marketed and own 88 per cent. of all anthracite deposits. The Morgan associates are the *nexus* between such supposedly competing railroads as the Northern Pacific and the Great Northern; the Southern, the Louisville & Nashville and the Atlantic Coast Line, and between partially competing industrials like the Westinghouse Electric and Manufacturing Company and the General Electric. The *nexus* between all the large potentially competing corporations must be severed, if the Money Trust is to be broken.

PROHIBITING CORPORATE CONTRACTS IN WHICH THE MANAGEMENT HAS A PRIVATE INTEREST

The principle of prohibiting corporate contracts in which the management has a private interest is applied, in the Pujo Committee's recommendations, only to national banks, and in them only to officers. All other corporations are to be permitted to continue the practice; and even in national banks the directors are to be free to have a conflicting private interest, except that they must not accept compensation for promoting a loan of bank funds nor participate in syndicates, promotions or underwriting of securities in which their banks may be interested as underwriters or owners or lenders thereon: that all loans or other transactions in which a director is interested shall be made in his own name; and shall be authorized only after ample notice to co-directors; and that the facts shall be spread upon the records of the corporation.

The Money Trust would not be disturbed by a prohibition limited to officers. Under a law of that character, financial control would continue to be exercised by the few without substantial impairment; but the power would be exerted through a somewhat different channel. Bank officers are appointees of the directors; and ordinarily their obedient servants. Individuals who, as bank officers, are now important factors in the financial concentration, would doubtless resign as officers and become merely directors. The loss of official salaries involved could be easily compensated. No member of the firm of J. P. Morgan & Co. is an officer in any one of the thirteen banking institutions with aggregate resources of $1,283,000,000, through which as directors they carry on their vast operations. A prohibition limited to officers would not affect the Morgan operations with these banking institutions. If there were minority representation on bank boards (which the Pujo Committee wisely advocates), such a provision might afford some protection to stockholders through the vigilance of the minority directors preventing the dominant directors using their power to the injury of the minority stockholders. But even then, the provision would not safeguard the public; and the primary purpose of Money Trust legislation is not to prevent directors from injuring stockholders; but to prevent their injuring the public through the intertwined control of the banks. No prohibition limited to officers will materially change this condition.

The prohibition of interlocking directorates, even if applied only to all banks and trust companies, would practically compel the Morgan representatives to resign from the directorates of the thirteen banking institutions with which they are connected, or from the directorates of all the railroads, express, steamship, public utility, manufacturing, and other corporations which do business with those banks and trust companies. Whether they resigned from the one or the other class of corporations, the endless chain would be broken into many pieces. And whether they retired or not, the Morgan power would obviously be greatly lessened: for if they did not retire, their field of operations would be greatly narrowed.

APPLY THE PRIVATE INTEREST PROHIBITION TO ALL KINDS OF CORPORATIONS

The creation of the Money Trust is due quite as much to the encroachment of the investment banker upon railroads, public service, industrial, and life-insurance companies, as to his control of banks and trust companies. Before the Money Trust can be broken, all these relations must be severed. And they cannot be severed unless corporations of each of these several classes are prevented from dealing with their own directors and with corporations in which those directors are interested. For instance: The most potent single source of J. P. Morgan & Co.'s power is the $162,500,000 deposits, including those of 78 inter-state railroad, public-service and industrial corporations, which the Morgan firm is free to use as it sees fit. The proposed prohibition, even if applied to all banking institutions, would not affect directly this great source of Morgan power. If, however, the prohibition is made to include railroad, public-service, and industrial corporations, as well as banking institutions, members of J. P. Morgan & Co. will quickly retire from substantially all boards of directors.

APPLY THE PRIVATE INTEREST PROHIBITION TO STOCKHOLDING INTERESTS

The prohibition against one corporation entering into transactions with another corporation in which one of its directors is also interested, should apply even if his interest in the second corporation is merely that of stockholder. A conflict of interests in a director may be just as serious where he is a stockholder only in the second corporation, as if he were also a director.

One of the annoying petty monopolies, concerning which evidence was taken by the Pujo Committee, is the exclusive privilege granted to the American Bank Note Company by the New York Stock Exchange. A recent $60,000,000 issue of New York City bonds was denied listing on the Exchange, because the city refused to submit to an exaction of $55,800 by the American Company for engraving the bonds, when the New York Bank Note Company would do the work equally well for $44,500. As tending to explain this extraordinary monopoly, it was shown that men prominent in the financial world were stockholders in the American Company. Among the largest stockholders was Mr. Morgan, with 6,000 shares. No member of the Morgan firm was a director of the American Company; but there was sufficient influence exerted somehow to give the American Company the stock exchange monopoly.

The Pujo Committee, while failing to recommend that transactions in which a director has a private interest be prohibited, recognizes that a stockholder's interest of more than a certain size may be as potent an instrument of influence as a direct personal interest; for it recommends that:

"Borrowings, directly or indirectly by . . . any corporation of the stock of which he (a bank director) holds upwards of 10 per cent. from the bank of which he is such director, should only be permitted, on condition that notice shall have been given to his co-directors and that a full statement of the transaction shall be entered upon the minutes of the meeting at which such loan was authorized."

As shown above, the particular provision for notice affords no protection to the public; but if it did, its application ought to be extended to lesser stock-holdings. Indeed it is difficult to fix a limit so low that financial interest will not influence action. Certainly a stockholding interest of a single director, much smaller than 10 per cent., might be most effective in inducing favors. Mr. Morgan's stockholdings in the American Bank Note Company was only three per cent. The $6,000,000 investment of J. P. Morgan & Co. in the National City Bank represented only 6 per cent. of the bank's stock; and would undoubtedly have been effective, even if it had not been supplemented by the election of his son to the board of directors.

SPECIAL DISQUALIFICATIONS

The Stanley Committee, after investigation of the Steel Trust, concluded that the evils of interlocking directorates were so serious that representatives of certain industries which are largely dependent upon railroads should be absolutely prohibited from serving as railroad directors, officers or employees. It, therefore, proposed to disqualify as railroad director, officer or employee any person engaged in the business of manufacturing or selling railroad cars or locomotives, railroad rail or structural steel, or in mining and selling coal. The drastic Stanley bill, shows how great is the desire to do away with present abuses and to lessen the power of the Money Trust.

Directors, officers, and employees of banking institutions should, by a similar provision, be disqualified from acting as directors, officers or employees of life-insurance companies.[6] The Armstrong investigation showed that life-insurance companies were in 1905 the most potent factor in financial concentration. Their power was exercised largely through the banks and trust companies which they controlled by stock ownership and their huge deposits. The Armstrong legislation directed life-insurance companies to sell their stocks. The Mutual Life and the Equitable did so in part. But the Morgan associates bought the stocks. And now, instead of the life-insurance companies controlling the banks and trust companies, the latter and the bankers control the life-insurance companies.

HOW THE PROHIBITION MAY BE LIMITED

The Money Trust cannot be destroyed unless all *classes* of corporations are included in the prohibition

[6] New York State Senator William W. Armstrong headed an investigation of life insurance companies in New York, September 5–December 30, 1905. Charles Evans Hughes served as special counsel to the Committee, a role that launched his political career.

of interlocking directors and of transactions by corporations in which the management has a private interest. But it does not follow that the prohibition must apply to *every* corporation of each class. Certain exceptions are entirely consistent with merely protecting the public against the Money Trust; although protection of minority stockholders and business ethics demand that the rule prohibiting a corporation from making contracts in which a director has a private financial interest should be universal in its application. The number of corporations in the United States Dec. 31, 1912, was 305,336. Of these only 1610 have a capital of more than $5,000,000. Few corporations (other than banks) with a capital of less than $5,000,-000 could appreciably affect general credit conditions either through their own operations or their affiliations. Corporations (other than banks) with capital resources of less than $5,000,000 might, therefore, be excluded from the scope of the statute for the present. The prohibition could also be limited so as not to apply to any industrial concern, regardless of the amount of capital and resources, doing only an intrastate business; as practically all large industrial corporations are engaged in interstate commerce. This would exclude some retail concerns and local jobbers and manufacturers not otherwise excluded from the operation of the act. Likewise banks and trust companies located in cities of less than 100,000 inhabitants might, if thought advisable, be excluded, for the present if their capital is less than $500,000, and their resources less than, say, $2,500,000. In larger cities even the smaller banking institutions should be subject to the law. Such exceptions should overcome any objection which might be raised that in some smaller cities, the prohibition of interlocking directorates would exclude from the bank directorates all the able business men of the community through fear of losing the opportunity of bank accommodations.

An exception should also be made, so as to permit interlocking directorates between a corporation and its proper subsidiaries. And the prohibition of transactions in which the management has a private interest should, of course, not apply to contracts, express or implied, for such services as are performed indiscriminately for the whole community by railroads and public service corporations, or for services, common to all customers, like the ordinary service of a bank for its depositors.

THE POWER OF CONGRESS

The question may be asked: Has Congress the power to impose these limitations upon the conduct of any business other than national banks? And if the power of Congress is so limited, will not the dominant financiers, upon the enactment of such a law, convert their national banks into state banks or trust companies, and thus escape from congressional control?

The answer to both questions is clear. Congress has ample power to impose such prohibitions upon practically all corporations, including state banks, trust companies and life insurance companies; and evasion may be made impossible. While Congress has not been granted power to regulate *directly* state banks, and trust or life insurance companies, or railroad, public-service and industrial corporations, except in respect to interstate commerce, it may do so *indirectly* by virtue either of its control of the mail privilege or through the taxing power.

Practically no business in the United States can be

conducted without use of the mails; and Congress may in its reasonable discretion deny the use of the mail to any business which is conducted under conditions deemed by Congress to be injurious to the public welfare. Thus, Congress has no power directly to suppress lotteries; but it has indirectly suppressed them by denying, under heavy penalty, the use of the mail to lottery enterprises. Congress has no power to suppress directly business frauds; but it is constantly doing so indirectly by issuing fraud-orders denying the mail privilege. Congress has no direct power to require a newspaper to publish a list of its proprietors and the amount of its circulation, or to require it to mark paid-matter distinctly as advertising: But it has thus regulated the press, by denying the second-class mail privilege, to all publications which fail to comply with the requirements prescribed.

The taxing power has been restored to by Congress for like purposes: Congress has no power to regulate the manufacture of matches, or the use of oleomargarine; but it has suppressed the manufacture of the "white phosphorous" match and has greatly lessened the use of oleomargarine by imposing heavy taxes upon them. Congress has no power to prohibit, or to regulate directly the issue of bank notes by state banks, but it indirectly prohibited their issue by imposing a tax of ten per cent. upon any bank note issued by a state bank.

The power of Congress over interstate commerce has been similarly utilized. Congress cannot ordinarily provide compensation for accidents to employees or undertake directly to suppress prostitution; but it has, as an incident of regulating interstate commerce, enacted the Railroad Employers' Liability law and the White Slave Law; and it has full power over the instrumentalities of commerce, like the telegraph and the telephone.

As such exercise of congressional power has been common for, at least, half a century, Congress should not hestitate now to employ it where its exercise is urgently needed. For a comprehensive prohibition of interlocking directorates is an essential condition of our attaining the New Freedom. Such a law would involve a great change in the relation of the leading banks and bankers to other businesses. But it is the very purpose of Money Trust legislation to effect a great change; and unless it does so, the power of our financial oligarchy cannot be broken.

But though the enactment of such a law is essential to the emancipation of business, it will not *alone* restore industrial liberty. It must be supplemented by other remedial measures.

CHAPTER V

WHAT PUBLICITY CAN DO

PUBLICITY is justly commended as a remedy for social and industrial diseases. Sunlight is said to be the best of disinfectants; electric light the most efficient policeman. And publicity has already played an important part in the struggle against the Money Trust. The Pujo Committee has, in the disclosure of the facts concerning financial concentration, made a most important contribution toward attainment of the New Freedom. The battlefield has been surveyed and charted. The hostile forces have been located, counted and appraised. That was a necessary first step—and a long one—towards relief. The provisions in the Committee's bill concerning the incorporation of stock exchanges and the statement to be made in connection with the listing of securities would doubtless have a beneficent effect. But there should be a further call upon publicity for service. That potent force must, in the impending struggle, be utilized in many ways as a continuous remedial measure.

WEALTH

Combination and control of other people's money and of other people's businesses. These are the main factors in the development of the Money Trust. But the wealth of the investment banker is also a factor. And with the extraordinary growth of his wealth in recent years, the relative importance of wealth as a factor in financial concentration has grown steadily. It was wealth which enabled Mr. Morgan, in 1910, to pay $3,000,000 for $51,000 par value of the stock of the Equitable Life Insurance Society. His direct income from this investment was limited by law to less than one-eighth of one per cent. a year; but it gave legal control of $504,000,000, of assets. It was wealth which enabled the Morgan associates to buy from the Equitable and the Mutual Life Insurance Company the stocks in the several banking institutions, which, merged in the Bankers' Trust Company and the Guaranty Trust Company, gave them control of $357,000,000 deposits. It was wealth which enabled Mr. Morgan to acquire his shares in the First National and National City banks, worth $21,000,000, through which he cemented the triple alliance with those institutions.

Now, how has this great wealth been accumulated? Some of it was natural accretion. Some of it is due to special opportunities for investment wisely availed of. Some of it is due to the vast extent of the bankers' operations. Then power breeds wealth as wealth breeds power. But a main cause of these large fortunes is the huge tolls taken by those who control the avenues to capital and to investors. There has been exacted as toll literally "all that the traffic will bear."

EXCESSIVE BANKERS' COMMISSIONS

The Pujo Committee was unfortunately prevented by lack of time from presenting to the country the evidence covering the amounts taken by the investment bankers as promoters' fees, underwriting commissions and profits. Nothing could have demonstrated so clearly the power exercised by the bankers, as a schedule showing the aggregate of these taxes levied within recent years. It would be well worth while now to reopen the Money Trust investigation merely to collect these data. But earlier investigations have disclosed some illuminating, though sporadic facts.

The syndicate which promoted the Steel Trust, took, as compensation for a few weeks' work, securities yielding $62,500,000 in cash; and of this, J. P. Morgan & Co. received for their services, as Syndicate Managers, $12,500,000, besides their share, as syndicate subscribers, in the remaining $50,000,000. The Morgan syndicate took for promoting the Tube Trust $20,000,000 common stock out of a total issue of $80,000,000 stock (preferred and common). Nor were monster commissions limited to trust promotions. More recently, bankers' syndicates have, in many instances, received for floating preferred stocks of recapitalized industrial concerns, one-third of all common stock issued, besides a considerable sum in

cash. And for the sale of preferred stock of well
established manufacturing concerns, cash commissions (or profits) of from 7½ to 10 per cent. of the
cash raised are often exacted. On bonds of high-class
industrial concerns, bankers' commissions (or profits)
of from 5 to 10 points have been common.

Nor have these heavy charges been confined to
industrial concerns. Even railroad securities, supposedly of high grade, have been subjected to like
burdens. At a time when the New Haven's credit
was still unimpaired, J. P. Morgan & Co. took the
New York, Westchester & Boston Railway first mort-
gage bonds, guaranteed by the New Haven at 92 1/2;
and they were marketed at 96 1/4. They took the Portland Terminal Company bonds, guaranteed by the
Maine Central Railroad—a corporation of unquestion-
able credit—at about 88, and these were marketed
at 92.

A large part of these underwriting commissions is
taken by the great banking houses, not for their services in selling the bonds, nor in assuming risks, but
for securing others to sell the bonds and incur risks.
Thus when the Interboro Railway—a most prosperous
corporation—financed its recent $170,000,000 bond
issue, J. P. Morgan & Co. received a 3 per cent commission, that is $5,100,000, practically for arranging
that others should underwrite and sell the bonds.

The aggregate commissions or profits so taken by
leading banking houses can only be conjectured, as the
full amount of their transactions has not been disclosed, and the rate of commission or profit varies very
widely. But the Pujo Committee has supplied some
interesting data bearing upon the subject: Counting
the issues of securities of interstate corporations only,
J. P. Morgan & Co. directly procured the public mar-

keting alone or in conjunction with others during the years 1902-1912, of $1,950,000,000. What the average commission or profit taken by J. P. Morgan & Co. was we do not know; but we do know that every one per cent on that sum yields $19,500,000. Yet even that huge aggregate of $1,950,000,000 includes only a part of the securities on which commissions or profits were paid. It does not include any issue of an intra-state corporation. It does not include any securities privately marketed. It does not include any government, state or municipal bonds.

It is to exactions such as these that the wealth of the investment banker is in large part due. And since this wealth is an important factor in the creation of the power exercised by the Money Trust, we must endeavor to put an end to this improper wealth getting, as well as to improper combination. The Money Trust is so powerful and so firmly entrenched, that each of the sources of its undue power must be effectually stopped, if we would attain the New Freedom.

HOW SHALL EXCESSIVE CHARGES BE STOPPED?

The Pujo Committee recommends, as a remedy for such excessive charges, that interstate corporations be prohibited from entering into any agreements creating a sole fiscal agent to dispose of their security issues; that the issue of the securities of interstate railroads be placed under the supervision of the Interstate Commerce Commission; and that their securities should be disposed of only upon public or private competitive bids, or under regulations to be prescribed by the Commission with full powers of investigation that will discover and punish combinations which prevent competition in bidding. Some of the state public-service commissions now exercise such power; and it may possibly be wise to confer this power upon the interstate commission, although the recommendation of the Hadley Railroad Securities Commission are to the contrary. [7] But the official regulation as proposed by the Pujo Committee would be confined to railroad corporations; and the new security issues of other corporations listed on the New York Stock Exchange have aggregated in the last five years $4,525,404,025, which is more than either the railroad or the municipal issues. Publicity offers, however, another and even more promising remedy: a method of regulating bankers' charges which would apply automatically to railroad, public-service and industrial corporations alike.

The question may be asked: Why have these excessive charges been submitted to? Corporations, which in the first instance bear the charges for capital, have, doubtless, submitted because of banker-control; exercised directly through interlocking directorates, or kindred relations, and indirectly through combinations among bankers to suppress competition. But why have the investors submitted, since ultimately all these charges are borne by the investors, except so far as corporations succeed in shifting the burden upon the community? The large army of small investors, constituting a substantial majority of all security buyers, are entirely free from banker control. Their submission is undoubtedly due, in part, to the fact that the bankers control the avenues to recognizedly safe investments almost as fully as they do the avenues to capital. But the investor's servility is due partly, also, to his ignorance of the facts. Is it not probable that, if each investor knew the extent to which the security he buys from the banker is diluted by excessive underwritings, commissions and profits, there would be a strike of capital against these unjust exactions?

---

[7] In 1910, Congress established a Railroad Securities Commission to

THE STRIKE OF CAPITAL

A recent British experience supports this view. In a brief period last spring nine different issues, aggregating $135,840,000, were offered by syndicates on the London market, and on the average only about 10 per cent of these loans was taken by the public. Money was "tight," but the rates of interest offered were very liberal, and no one doubted that the investors were well supplied with funds. *The London Daily Mail* presented an explanation:

"The long series of rebuffs to new loans at the hands of investors reached a climax in the ill success of the great Rothschild issue. It will remain a topic of financial discussion for many days, and many in the city are expressing the opinion that it may have a revolutionary effect upon the present system of loan issuing and underwriting. The question being discussed is that the public have become loth to subscribe for stock which they believe the underwriters can afford, by reason of the commission they receive, to sell subsequently at a lower price than the issue price, and that the Stock Exchange has begun to realize the public's attitude. The public sees in the underwriter not so much one who insures that the loan shall be subscribed in return for its commission as a middleman, who, as it were, has an opportunity of obtaining stock at a lower price than the public in order that he may pass it off at a profit subsequently. They prefer not to subscribe, but to await an opportunity of dividing that profit. They feel that if, when these issues were made, the stock were offered them at a more attractive price, there would be less need to pay the underwriters so high commissions. It is another practical protest, if indirect,

study how Congress might regulate railroad finance. Taft named Arthur T. Hadley, President of Yale, to head the Commission, which was dominated by conservatives. Its Report, issued in November 1911, 1) rejected proposals for Federal regulation of railroad securities

against the existence of the middleman, which protest is one of the features of present-day finance."

PUBLICITY AS A REMEDY

Compel bankers when issuing securities to make public the commissions or profits they are receiving. Let
every circular letter, prospectus or advertisement of a
bond or stock show clearly what the banker received
for his middleman-services, and what the bonds and
stocks net the issuing corporation. That is knowledge
to which both the existing security holder and the prospective purchaser is fairly entitled. If the bankers'
compensation is reasonable, considering the skill and
risk involved, there can be no objection to making it
known. If it is not reasonable, the investor will
"strike," as investors seem to have done recently in
England.

Such disclosures of bankers' commissions or profits
is demanded also for another reason: It will aid the
investor in judging of the safety of the investment. In
the marketing of securities there are two classes of
risks: One is the risk whether the banker (or the corporation) will find ready purchasers for the bonds or
stock at the issue price; the other whether the investor will get a good article. The maker of the security
and the banker are interested chiefly in getting it sold
at the issue price. The investor is interested chiefly
in buying a good article. The small investor relies almost exclusively upon the banker for his knowledge
and judgment as to the quality of the security; and it
is this which makes his relation to the banker one of
confidence. But at present, the investment banker oc-
cupies a position inconsistent with that relation. The
bankers' compensation should, of course, vary according

(at least until the Supreme Court more clearly defined the relations
of state and Federal authority on the matter), 2) argued that there
was little relationship between capitalization and railroad rates (a

to the risk *he* assumes. Where there is a large risk that
the bonds or stock will not be promptly sold at the issue
price, the underwriting commission (that is the insurance premium) should be correspondingly large. But
the banker ought not to be paid more for getting *investors* to assume a larger risk. In practice the banker
gets the higher commission for underwriting the weaker
security, on the ground that his own risk is greater.
And the weaker the security, the greater is the banker's incentive to induce his customers to relieve him.
Now the law should not undertake (except incidentally
in connection with railroads and public-service corporations) to fix bankers' profits. And it should not seek
to prevent investors from making bad bargains. But
it is now recognized in the simplest merchandising,
that there should be full disclosures. The archaic doctrine of *caveat emptor* is vanishing. The law has begun
to require publicity in aid of fair dealing. The Federal Pure Food Law does not guarantee quality or
prices; but it helps the buyer to judge of quality by requiring disclosure of ingredients. Among the most
important facts to be learned for determining the real
value of a security is the amount of water it contains.
And any excessive amount paid to the banker for marketing a security is water. Require a full disclosure to
the investor of the amount of commissions and profits
paid; and not only will investors be put on their guard,
but bankers' compensation will tend to adjust itself
automatically to what is fair and reasonable. Excessive
commissions—this form of unjustly acquired wealth—
will in large part cease.

REAL DISCLOSURE

But the disclosure must be real. And it must be a
disclosure to the investor. It will not suffice to require

---

view hotly disputed by progressives then and since), 3) recommended
that railroads be permitted to issue "No Par" stock (a proposal
economist and railroad specialist William Z. Ripley of Harvard con-

merely the filing of a statement of facts with the Commissioner of Corporations or with a score of other officials, federal and state. That would be almost as ineffective as if the Pure Food Law required a manufacturer merely to deposit with the Department a statement of ingredients, instead of requiring the label to tell the story. Nor would the filing of a full statement with the Stock Exchange, if incorporated, as provided by the Pujo Committee bill, be adequate.

To be effective, knowledge of the facts must be actually brought home to the investor, and this can best be done by requiring the facts to be stated in good, large type in every notice, circular, letter and advertisement inviting the investor to purchase. Compliance with this requirement should also be obligatory, and not something which the investor could waive. For the whole public is interested in putting an end to the bankers' exactions. England undertook, years ago, to protect its investors against the wiles of promoters, by requiring a somewhat similar disclosure; but the British act failed, in large measure of its purpose, partly because under it the statement of facts was filed only with a public official, and partly because the investor could waive the provision. And the British statute has now been changed in the latter respect.

The required publicity should also include a dis-

DISCLOSE SYNDICATE PARTICULARS

closure of all participants in an underwriting. It is a common incident of underwriting that no member of the syndicate shall sell at less than the syndicate price for a definite period, unless the syndicate is sooner dissolved. In other words, the bankers make, by agreement, an artificial price. Often the agreement is prob-

---

tended would "revolutionize all of our customary habits of financial thought"), and 4) suggested that publicity about a railroad's physical evaluation and of its securities outstanding would provide sufficient control of railroad financial practices.

ably illegal under the Sherman Anti-Trust Law. This price maintenance is, however, not necessarily objectionable. It may be entirely consistent with the general welfare, if the facts are made known. But disclosure should include a list of those participating in the underwriting so that the public may not be misled. The investor should know whether his adviser is disinterested.

Not long ago a member of a leading banking house was undertaking to justify a commission taken by his firm for floating a now favorite preferred stock of a manufacturing concern. The bankers took for their services $250,000 in cash, besides one-third of the common stock, amounting to about $2,000,000. "Of course," he said, "that would have been too much if we could have kept it all for ourselves; but we couldn't. We had to divide up a large part. There were fifty-seven participants. Why, we had even to give $10,000 of stock to————(naming the president of a leading bank in the city where the business was located). He might some day have been asked what he thought of the stock. If he had shrugged his shoulders and said he didn't know, we might have lost many a customer for the stock. We had to give him $10,000 of the stock to teach him not to shrug his shoulders."

Think of the effectiveness with practical Americans of a statement like this:

A. B. & CO.

Investment Bankers

We have today secured substantial control of the successful machinery business heretofore conducted by ———— at ————, Illinois, which has been incorporated under the name of the Excelsior Manufacturing Company with a capital of $10,000,000, of which $5,000,000 is Preferred and $5,000,000 Common.

As we have a large clientele of confiding customers, we were able to secure from the owners an agreement for marketing the Preferred stock—we to fix a price which shall net the owners in cash $95 a share.

We offer this excellent stock to you at $100.75 per share. Our own commission or profit will be only a little over $5.00 per share, or say, $250,000 cash besides $1,500,000 of the Common stock, which we received as a bonus. This cash and stock commission we are to divide in various proportions with the following participants in the underwriting syndicate:

C. D. & Co., New York
E. F. & Co., Boston
L. M. & Co., Philadelphia
I. K. & Co., New York
O. P. & Co., Chicago

Were such notices common, the investment bankers would "be worthy of their hire," for only reasonable compensation would ordinarily be taken.

For marketing the preferred stock, as in the case of Excelsior Manufacturing Co. referred to above, investment bankers were doubtless essential, and as middlemen they performed a useful service. But they used their strong position to make an excessive charge. There are, however, many cases where the banker's services can be altogether dispensed with; and where that is possible he should be eliminated, not only for economy's sake, but to break up financial concentration.

CHAPTER VI

WHERE THE BANKER IS SUPERFLUOUS

THE abolition of interlocking directorates will greatly curtail the bankers' power by putting an end to many improper combinations. Publicity concerning bankers' commissions, profits and associates, will lend effective aid, particularly by curbing undue exactions. Many of the specific measures recommended by the Pujo Committee (some of them dealing with technical details) will go far toward correcting corporate and banking abuses; and thus tend to arrest financial concentration. But the investment banker has, within his legitimate province, acquired control so extensive as to menace the public welfare even where his business is properly conducted. If the New Freedom is to be attained, every proper means of lessening that power must be availed of. A simple and effective remedy, which can be widely applied, even without new legislation, lies near at hand:—Eliminate the banker-middleman where he is superfluous.

Today practically all governments, states and municipalities pay toll to the banker on all bonds sold. Why should they? It is not because the banker is always needed. It is because the banker controls the only avenue through which the investor in bonds and stocks can ordinarily be reached. The banker has become the universal tax gatherer. True, the *pro rata* of taxes levied by him upon our state and city governments is less than that levied by him upon the corporations. But few states or cities escape payment of some such tax to the banker on every loan it makes. Even where the new issues of bonds are sold at public auction, or to the highest bidder on sealed proposals, the bankers' syndicates usually secure large blocks of the bonds which are sold to the people at a considerable profit. The middleman, even though unnecessary, collects his tribute.

There is a legitimate field for dealers in state and municipal bonds, as for other merchants. Investors already owning such bonds must have a medium through which they can sell their holdings. And those states or municipalities which lack an established reputation among investors, or which must seek more distant markets, need the banker to distribute new issues. But there are many states and cities which have an established reputation and have a home market at hand. These should sell their bonds direct to investors without the intervention of a middleman. And as like conditions prevail with some corporations, their bonds and stocks should also be sold direct to the investor. Both financial efficiency and industrial liberty demand that the bankers' toll be abolished, where that is possible.

BANKER AND BROKER

The business of the investment banker must not be confused with that of the bond and stock broker. The two are often combined; but the functions are essentially different. The broker performs a very limited service. He has properly nothing to do with the original issue of securities, nor with their introduction into the market. He merely negotiates a purchase or sale as agent for another under specific orders. He exercises no discretion, except in the method of bringing buyer and seller together, or of executing orders. For his humble service he receives a moderate compensation, a commission, usually one-eighth of one per cent. (12 1/2

cents for each $100) on the par value of the security
sold. The investment banker also is a mere middleman. But he is a principal, not an agent. He is also
a merchant in bonds and stocks. The compensation
received for his part in the transaction is in many
cases more accurately described as profit than as commission. So far as concerns new issues of government, state and municipal bonds, especially, he acts as
merchant, buying and selling securities on his own
behalf; buying commonly at wholesale from the maker
and selling at retail to the investors; taking the merchant's risk and the merchant's profits. On purchases
of corporate securities the profits are often very large;
but even a large profit may be entirely proper; for
when the banker's services are needed and are properly
performed, they are of great value. On purchases of
government, state and municipal securities the profit is
usually smaller; but even a very small profit cannot be
justified, if unnecessary.

HOW THE BANKER CAN SERVE

The banker's services include three distinct functions, and only three:

First: Specifically as expert. The investment banker
has the responsibility of the ordinary retailer to sell
only that merchandise which is good of its kind. But
his responsibility in this respect is unusually heavy,
because he deals in an article on which a great majority
of his customers are unable, themselves, to pass intelligent judgment without aid. The purchase by the investor of most corporate securities is little better than
a gamble, where he fails to get the advice of some one
who has investigated the security thoroughly as the
banker should. For few investors have the time, the

facilities, or the ability to investigate properly the value of corporate securities.

Second: Specifically as distributor. The banker performs an all-important service in providing an outlet for securities. His connections enable him to reach possible buyers quickly. And good-will—that is, possession of the confidence of regular customers—enables him to effect sales where the maker of the security might utterly fail to find a market.

Third: Specifically as jobber or retailer. The investment banker, like other merchants, carries his stock in trade until it can be marketed. In this he performs a service which is often of great value to the maker. Needed cash is obtained immediately, because the whole issue of securities can thus be disposed of by a single transaction. And even where there is not immediate payment, the knowledge that the money will be provided when needed is often of paramount importance. By carrying securities in stock, the banker performs a service also to investors, who are thereby enabled to buy securities at such times as they desire.

Whenever makers of securities or investors require all or any of these three services, the investment banker is needed, and payment of compensation to him is proper. Where there is no such need, the banker is clearly superfluous. And in respect to the original issue of many of our state and municipal bonds, and of some corporate securities, no such need exists.

WHERE THE BANKER SERVES NOT

It needs no banker experts in value to tell us that bonds of Massachusetts or New York, of Boston, Philadelphia or Baltimore and of scores of lesser American cities, are safe investments. The basic financial facts in regard to such bonds are a part of the common knowledge of many American investors; and, certainly, of most possible investors who reside in the particular state or city whose bonds are in question. Where the financial facts are not generally known, they are so simple, that they can be easily summarized and understood by any prospective investor without interpretation by an expert. Bankers often employ, before purchasing securities, their own accountants to verify the statements supplied by the makers of the security, and use these accountants' certificates as an aid in selling. States and municipalities, the makers of the securities, might for the same purpose employ independent public accountants of high reputation, who would give their certificates for use in marketing the securities. Investors could also be assured without banker-aid that the basic legal conditions are sound. Bankers, before purchasing an issue of securities, customarily obtain from their own counsel an opinion as to its legality, which investors are invited to examine. It would answer the same purpose, if states and municipalities should supplement the opinion of their legal representatives by that of independent counsel of recognized professional standing, who would certify to the legality of the issue.

Neither should an investment banker be needed to find investors willing to take up, in small lots, a new issue of bonds of New York or Massachusetts, of Boston, Philadelphia or Baltimore, or a hundred other American cities. A state or municipality seeking to market direct to the investor its own bonds would naturally experience, at the outset, some difficulty in marketing a large issue. And in a newer community, where there is little accumulation of unemployed capital, it might be impossible to find buyers for any large issue. Investors are apt to be conservative; and they have been trained to regard the intervention of the banker as necessary. The bankers would naturally discourage any attempt of states and cities to dispense with their services. Entrance upon a market, hitherto monopolized by them, would usually have to be struggled for. But banker-fed investors, as well as others could, in time, be brought to realize the advantage of avoiding the middleman and dealing directly with responsible borrowers. Governments, like private concerns, would have to do educational work; but this publicity would be much less expensive and much more productive than that undertaken by the bankers. Many investors are already impatient of banker exactions; and eager to deal directly with governmental agencies in whom they have more confidence. And a great demand could, at once, be developed among smaller investors whom the bankers have been unable to interest, and who now never buy state or municipal bonds. The opening of this new field would furnish a market, in some respects more desirable and certainly wider than that now reached by the bankers.

Neither do states or cities ordinarily need the services of the investment banker to carry their bonds pending distribution to the investor. Where there is immediate need for large funds, states and cities—at least the older communities—should be able to raise the money temporarily, quite as well as the bankers do now, while awaiting distribution of their bonds to the investor. Bankers carry the bonds with other people's money, not with their own. Why should not cities get the temporary use of other people's money as well? Bankers have the preferential use of the deposits in the banks, often because they control the banks. Free [8] these institutions from banker-control, and no appli-

---

[8] This sentence should read: "*Investment* bankers have the preferential use of the deposits in the banks, often because they control the banks *of deposit*."

cant to borrow the people's money will be received with greater favor than our large cities. Boston, with its $1,500,000,000 of assessed valuation and $78,033,128 net debt, is certainly as good a risk as even Lee, Higginson & Co. or Kidder, Peabody & Co.

But ordinarily cities do not, or should not, require large sums of money at any one time. Such need of large sums does not arise except from time to time where maturing loans are to be met, or when some existing public utility plant is to be taken over from private owners. Large issues of bonds for any other purpose are usually made in anticipation of future needs, rather than to meet present necessities. Modern efficient public financiering, through substituting serial bonds for the long term issues (which in Massachusetts has been made obligatory) will, in time, remove the need of large sums at one time for paying maturing debts, since each year's maturities will be paid from the year's taxes. Purchases of existing public utility plants are of rare occurrence, and are apt to be preceded by long periods of negotiations. When they occur they can, if foresight be exercised, usually be financed without full cash payment at one time.

Today, when a large issue of bonds is made, the banker, while ostensibly paying his own money to the city, actually pays to the city other people's money which he has borrowed from the banks. Then the banks get back, through the city's deposits, a large part of the money so received. And when the money is returned to the bank, the banker has the opportunity of borrowing it again for other operations. The process results in double loss to the city. The city loses by not getting from the banks as much for its bonds as investors would pay. And then it loses interest on the money raised before it is needed. For the bankers

receive from the city bonds bearing rarely less than
4 per cent. interest; while the proceeds are deposited
in the banks which rarely allow more than 2 per cent.
interest on the daily balances.

CITIES THAT HAVE HELPED THEMSELVES

In the present year some cities have been led by
necessity to help themselves. The bond market was
poor. Business was uncertain, money tight and the
ordinary investor reluctant. Bankers were loth to take
new bond issues. Municipalities were unwilling to pay
the high rates demanded of them. And many cities
were prohibited by law or ordinance from paying more
than 4 per cent. interest; while good municipal bonds
were selling on a 4 1/2 to 5 per cent. basis. But money
had to be raised, and the attempt was made to borrow
it direct from the lenders instead of from the banker-
middleman. Among the cities which raised money in
this way were Philadelphia, Baltimore, St. Paul, and
Utica, New York.

Philadelphia, under Mayor Blankenburg's inspira- [9]
tion, sold nearly $4,175,000 in about two days on a 4
per cent. basis and another "over-the-counter" sale has
been made since. In Baltimore, with the assistance of
the *Sun,* $4,766,000 were sold "over the counter" on
a 4 1/2 per cent. basis. Utica's two "popular sales" of
4 1/2 per cent. bonds were largely "over-subscribed."
And since then other cities large and small have had
their "over-the-counter" bond sales. The experience
of Utica, as stated by its Controller, Fred G. Reusswig,
must prove of general interest:

"In June of the present year I advertised for sale
two issues, one of $100,000, and the other of $19,000,
bearing interest at 4 1/2 per cent. The latter issue was

[9] Rudolph Blankenburg, an elderly German-American immigrant,
was elected mayor of Philadelphia in 1912 when a wave of anti-machine
insurgency within the G.O.P. split the party and gave the Democrats
brief control of the city.

purchased at par by a local bidder and of the former
we purchased $10,000 for our sinking funds. That
left $90,000 unsold, for which there were no bidders,
which was the first time that I had been unable to sell
our bonds. About this time the 'popular sales' of Baltimore and Philadelphia attracted my attention. The
laws in effect in those cities did not restrict the officials
as does our law and I could not copy their methods. I
realized that there was plenty of money in this immediate vicinity and if I could devise a plan conforming
with our laws under which I could make the sale attractive to small investors it would undoubtedly prove successful. I had found, in previous efforts to interest
people of small means, that they did not understand the
meaning of premium and would rather not buy than
bid above par. They also objected to making a deposit
with their bids. In arranging for the 'popular sales' I
announced in the papers that, while I must award to
the highest bidder, it was my opinion that a par bid
would be *the highest bid*. I also announced that we
would issue bonds in denominations as low as $100 and
that we would not require a deposit except where the
bid was $5,000 or over. Then I succeeded in getting
the local papers to print editorials and local notices
upon the subject of municipal bonds, with particular
reference to those of Utica and the forthcoming sale.
All the prospective purchaser had to do was to fill in the
amount desired, sign his name, seal the bid and await
the day for the award. I did not have many bidders for
very small amounts. There was only one for $100 at
the first sale and one for $100 at the second sale and
not more than ten who wanted less than $500. Most
of the bidders were looking for from $1,000 to $5,000,
but nearly all were people of comparatively small
means, and with some the investment represented all

their savings. In awarding the bonds I gave preference to residents of Utica and I had no difficulty in apportioning the various maturities in a satisfactory way.

"I believe that there are a large number of persons in every city who would buy their own bonds if the way were made easier by law. Syracuse and the neighboring village of Ilion, both of which had been unable to sell in the usual way, came to me for a program of procedure and both have since had successful sales along similar lines. We have been able by this means to keep the interest rate on our bonds at 4 1/2 per cent., while cities which have followed the old plan of relying upon bond houses have had to increase the rate to 5 per cent. I am in favor of amending the law in such a manner that the Common Council, approved by the Board of Estimate and Apportionment, may fix the prices at which bonds shall be sold, instead of calling for competitive bids Then place the bonds on sale at the Controller's office to any one who will pay the price. The prices upon each issue should be graded according to the different values of different maturities. Under the present law, as we have it, conditions are too complicated to make a sale practicable except upon a basis of par bids."

THE ST. PAUL EXPERIMENT

St. Paul wisely introduced into its experiment a more democratic feature, which Tom L. Johnson, Cleveland's great mayor, thought out (but did not utilize), and which his friend W. B. Colver, now Editor-in-Chief of the *Daily News*, brought to the attention of the St. Paul officials. Mayor Johnson had recognized the importance of reaching the small savings of the people; and concluded that it was necessary not only to issue the bonds in very small denominations, but also to make them redeemable at par. He sought to combine practically, bond investment with the savings bank privilege. The fact that municipal bonds are issuable ordinarily only in large denominations, say, $1,000, presented an obstacle to be overcome. Mayor Johnson's plan was to have the sinking fund commissioners take large blocks of the bonds, issue against them certificates in denominations of $10, and have the commissioners agree (under their power to purchase securities) to buy the certificates back at par and interest. Savings bank experience, he insisted, showed that the redemption feature would not prove an embarrassment; as the percentage of those wishing to withdraw their money is small; and deposits are nearly always far in excess of withdrawals.

The St. Paul sinking fund commissioners and City Attorney O'Neill approved the Johnson plan; and in the face of high money rates, sold on a 4 per cent. basis, during July, certificates to the net amount of $502,300; during August, $147,000; and during September, over $150,000, the average net sales being about $5,700 a day. Mr. Colver, reporting on the St. Paul experience, said:

"There have been about 2,000 individual purchasers making the average deposit about $350 or $360. There have been no certificates sold to banks. During the first month the deposits averaged considerably higher and for this reason: in very many cases people who had savings which represented the accumulation of considerable time, withdrew their money from the postal savings banks, from the regular banks, from various hiding places and deposited them with the city. Now these same people are coming once or twice a month and making deposits of ten or twenty dollars, so that the average of the individual deposit has fallen very rapidly during September and every indication is that the number of small deposits will continue to increase and the relatively large deposits become less frequent as time goes on.

As a matter of fact, these certificate deposits are stable, far more than the deposits and investments of richer people who watch for advantageous reinvestments and who shift their money about rather freely. The man with three or four hundred dollars savings will suffer almost anything before he will disturb that fund. We believe that the deposits every day here, day in and day out, will continue to take care of all the withdrawals and still leave a net gain for the day, that net figure at present being about $5,700 a day."

Many cities are now prevented from selling bonds direct to the small investors, through laws which compel bonds to be issued in large denominations or which require the issue to be offered to the highest bidder. These legislative limitations should be promptly removed.

SALESMANSHIP AND EDUCATION

Such success as has already been attained is largely due to the unpaid educational work of leading progressive newspapers. But the educational work to be done must not be confined to teaching "the people"—the buyers of the bonds. Municipal officials and legislators have quite as much to learn. They must, first of all, study salesmanship. Selling bonds to the people is a new art, still undeveloped. The general problems have not yet been worked out. And besides these problems common to all states and cities, there will be, in nearly every community, local problems which must be solved,

and local difficulties which must be overcome. The
proper solution even of the general problems must take
considerable time. There will have to be many experi-
ments made; and doubtless there will be many failures.
Every great distributor of merchandise knows the ob-
stacles which he had to overcome before success was
attained; and the large sums that had to be invested in
opening and preparing a market. Individual concerns
have spent millions in wise publicity; and have ultimately reaped immense profits when the market was
won. Cities must take their lessons from these great
distributors. Cities must be ready to study the problems
and to spend prudently for proper publicity work. It
might, in the end, prove an economy, even to allow,
on particular issues, where necessary, a somewhat
higher interest rate than bankers would exact, if thereby a direct market for bonds could be secured. Future
operations would yield large economies. And the obtaining of a direct market for city bonds is growing
ever more important, because of the huge increase in
loans which must attend the constant expansion of
municipal functions. In 1898 the new municipal issues
aggregated $103,084,793; in 1912, $380,810,287.

SAVINGS BANKS AS CUSTOMERS

In New York, Massachusetts and the other sixteen
states where a system of purely mutual savings banks
is general, it is possible, with a little organization, to
develop an important market for the direct purchaser
of bonds. The bonds issued by Massachusetts cities and
towns have averaged recently about $15,000,000 a year,
and those of the state about $3,000,000. The 194
Massachusetts savings banks, with aggregate assets of
$902,105,755.94, held on October 31, 1912, $90,536,-

581.32 in bonds and notes of states and municipalities. Of this sum about $60,000,000 are invested in bonds and notes of Massachusetts cities and towns, and about $8,000,000 in state issues. The deposits in the savings banks are increasing at the rate of over $30,000,000 a year. Massachusetts state and municipal bonds have, within a few years, come to be issued tax exempt in the hands of the holder, whereas other classes of bonds usually held by savings banks are subject to a tax of one-half of one per cent. of the market value. Massachusetts savings banks, therefore, will to an increasing extent, select Massachusetts municipal issues for high-grade bond investments. Certainly Massachusetts cities and towns might, with the coöperation of the Commonwealth, easily develop a "home market" for "over-the-counter" bond business with the savings banks. And the savings banks of other states offer similar opportunities to their municipalities.

COOPERATION

Bankers obtained their power through combination. Why should not cities and states by means of coöperation free themselves from the bankers? For by coöperation between the cities and the state, the direct marketing of municipal bonds could be greatly facilitated.

Massachusetts has 33 cities, each with a population of over 12,000 persons; 71 towns each with a population of over 5,000; and 250 towns each with a population of less than 5,000. Three hundred and eight of these municipalities now have funded indebtedness outstanding. The aggregate net indebtedness is about $180,000,000. Every year about $15,000,000 of bonds and notes are issued by the Massachusetts cities and towns for the purpose of meeting new requirements and refunding old indebtedness. If these municipalities would coöperate in marketing securities, the market for the bonds of each municipality would be widened; and there would exist also a common market for Massachusetts municipal securities which would be usually well supplied, would receive proper publicity and would attract investors. Successful merchandising obviously involves carrying an adequate, well-assorted stock. If every city acts alone, in endeavoring to market its bonds direct, the city's bond-selling activity will necessarily be sporadic. Its ability to supply the investor will be limited by its own necessities for money. The market will also be limited to the bonds of the particular municipality. But if a state and its cities should cooperate, there could be developed a continuous and broad market for the sale of bonds "over-the-counter." The joint selling agency of over three hundred municipalities,—as in Massachusetts—would naturally have a constant supply of assorted bonds and notes which could be had in as small amounts as the investor might want to buy them. It would be a simple matter to establish such a joint selling agency by which municipalities, under proper regulation of, and aid from the state, would coöperate.

And coöperation among the cities and with the state might serve in another important respect. These 354 Massachusetts municipalities carry in the aggregate large bank balances. Sometimes the balance carried by a city represents unexpended revenues; sometimes unexpended proceeds of loans. On these balances they usually receive from the banks 2 per cent. interest. The balances of municipalities vary like those of other depositors; one having idle funds, when another is in need. Why should not all of these cities and towns coöperate, making, say, the State their common banker, and supply each other with funds as farmers and laborers coöperate through credit unions? Then cities would get, instead of 2 per cent. on their balances, all their money was worth.

The Commonwealth of Massachusetts holds now in its sinking and other funds nearly $30,000,000 of Massachusetts municipal securities, constituting nearly three-fourth of all securities held in these funds. Its annual purchases aggregate nearly $4,000,000. Its purchases direct from cities and towns have already exceeded $1,000,000 this year. It would be but a simple extension of the state's function to coöperate, as indicated, in a joint, Municipal Bond Selling Agency and Credit Union. It would be a distinct advance in the efficiency of state and municipal financing; and what is even more important, a long step toward the emancipation of the people from banker-control.

CORPORATE SELF-HELP

Strong corporations with established reputations, locally or nationally, could emancipate themselves from the banker in a similar manner. Public-service corporations in some of our leading cities could easily establish "over-the-counter" home markets for their bonds; and would be greatly aided in this by the supervision now being exercised by some state commissions over the issue of securities by such corporations. Such corporations would gain thereby not only in freedom from banker-control and exactions, but in the winning of valuable local support. The investor's money would be followed by his sympathy. In things economic, as well as in things political, wisdom and safety lie in direct appeals to the people.

The Pennsylvania Railroad now relies largely upon its stockholders for new capital. But a corporation with its long-continued success and reputation for stability should have much wider financial support and should eliminate the banker altogether. With the 2,700 stations on its system, the Pennsylvania could, with a slight expense, create nearly as many avenues through which money would be obtainable to meet its growing needs.

BANKER PROTECTORS

It may be urged that reputations often outlive the conditions which justify them, that outlived reputations are pitfalls to the investors; and that the investment banker is needed to guard him from such dangers. True; but when have the big bankers or their little satellites protected the people from such pitfalls?

Was there ever a more be-bankered railroad than the New Haven? Was there ever a more banker-led community of investors than New England? Six years before the fall of that great system, the hidden dangers were pointed out to these banker-experts.[10] Proof was furnished of the rotting timbers. The disaster-breeding policies were laid bare. The bankers took no action. Repeatedly, thereafter, the bankers' attention was called to the steady deterioration of the structure. The New Haven books disclose 11,481 stockholders who are residents of Massachusetts · 5,682 stockholders in Connecticut; 735 in Rhode Island; and 3,510 in New York. Of the New Haven stockholders 10,474 were women. Of the New Haven stockholders 10,222 were of such modest means that their holdings were from one to ten shares only. The investors were sorely in need of protection. The city directories disclose 146

---

[10] Brandeis uses the passive tense to affect modesty; he refers actually to his own exposure of the New Haven's financial condition in 1907.

banking houses in Boston, 26 in Providence, 33 in New Haven and Hartford and 357 in New York City. But who, connected with those New England and New York banking houses, during the long years which preceded the recent investigation of the Interstate Commerce Commission, raised either voice or pen in protest against the continuous mismanagement of that great trust property or warned the public of the impending disaster? Some of the bankers sold their own stock holdings. Some bankers whispered to a few favored customers advice to dispose of New Haven stock. But not one banker joined those who sought to open the eyes of New England to the impending disaster and to avert it by timely measures. New England's leading banking houses were ready to "coôperate" with the New Haven management in taking generous commissions for marketing the endless supply of new securities; but they did nothing to protect the investors. Were these bankers blind? Or were they afraid to oppose the will of J. P. Morgan & Co.?

Perhaps it is the banker who, most of all, needs the New Freedom.

CHAPTER VII

BIG MEN AND LITTLE BUSINESS

J. P. Morgan & Co. declare, in their letter to the Pujo Committee, that "practically all the railroad and industrial development of this country has taken place initially through the medium of the great banking houses." That statement is entirely unfounded in fact. On the contrary nearly every such contribution to our comfort and prosperity was "initiated" *without* their aid. The "great banking houses" came into relation with these enterprises, either after success had been attained, or upon "reorganization" after the possibility of success had been demonstrated, but the funds of the hardy pioneers, who had risked their all, were exhausted.

This is true of our early railroads, of our early street railways, and of the automobile; of the telegraph, the telephone and the wireless; of gas and oil; of harvesting machinery, and of our steel industry; of textile, paper and shoe industries; and of nearly every other important branch of manufacture. The *initiation* of each of these enterprises may properly be characterized as "great transactions"; and the men who contributed the financial aid and business management necessary for their introduction are entitled to share, equally with inventors, in our gratitude for what has been accomplished. But the instances are extremely rare where the original financing of such enterprises was undertaken by investment bankers, great or small. It was usually done by some common business man, accustomed to taking risks; or by some well-to-do friend of the inventor or pioneer, who was influenced largely by considerations other than money-getting. Here and there you will find that banker-aid was given; but usually in those cases it was a small local banking concern, not a "great banking house" which helped to "initiate" the undertaking.

RAILROADS

We have come to associate the great bankers with railroads. But their part was not conspicuous in the early history of the Eastern railroads; and in the Middle West the experience was, to some extent, similar.

The Boston & Maine Railroad owns and leases 2,215
miles of line; but it is a composite of about 166 separate railroad companies. The New Haven Railroad
owns and leases 1,996 miles of line; but it is a composite of 112 separate railroad companies. The necessary capital to build these little roads was gathered
together, partly through state, county or municipal
aid; partly from business men or landholders who
sought to advance their special interests; partly from
investors; and partly from well-to-do public-spirited
men, who wished to promote the welfare of their particular communities. About seventy-five years after
the first of these railroads was built, J. P. Morgan &
Co. became fiscal agent for all of them by creating the
New Haven-Boston & Maine monopoly.

STEAMSHIPS

The history of our steamship lines is similar. In
1807, Robert Fulton, with the financial aid of Robert
R. Livingston, a judge and statesman—not a banker—
demonstrated with the *Claremont,* that it was practicable to propel boats by steam. In 1833 the three Cunard
brothers of Halifax and 232 other persons—stockholders of the Quebec and Halifax Steam Navigation Company—joined in supplying about $80,000 to build the
Royal William,—the first steamer to cross the Atlantic.
In 1902, many years after individual enterprises had
developed practically all the great ocean lines, J. P.
Morgan & Co. floated the International Mercantile
Marine with its $52,744,000 of 4 1/2 bonds, now sell-
ing at about 60, and $100,000,000 of stock (preferred
and common) on which no dividend has ever been paid.
It was just sixty-two years after the first regular line
of transatlantic steamers—The Cunard—was founded
that Mr. Morgan organized the Shipping Trust.

TELEGRAPH

The story of the telegraph is similar. The money for developing Morse's invention was supplied by his partner and co-worker, Alfred Vail. The initial line (from Washington to Baltimore) was built with an appropriation of $30,000 made by Congress in 1843. Sixty-six years later J. P. Morgan & Co. became bankers for the Western Union through financing its purchase by the American Telephone & Telegraph Company.

HARVESTING MACHINERY

Next to railroads and steamships, harvesting machinery has probably been the most potent factor in the development of America; and most important of the harvesting machines was Cyrus H. McCormick's reaper. That made it possible to increase the grain harvest twenty- or thirty-fold. No investment banker had any part in introducing this great business man's invention.

McCormick was without means; but William Butler Ogden, a railroad builder, ex-Mayor and leading citizen of Chicago, supplied $25,000 with which the first factory was built there in 1847. Fifty-five years later, J. P. Morgan & Co. performed the service of combining the five great harvester companies, and received a commission of $3,000,000. The concerns then consolidated as the International Harvester Company, with a capital stock of $120,000,000, had, despite their huge assets and earning power, been previously capitalized, in the aggregate, at only $10,500,000—strong evidence that in all the preceding years no investment

banker had financed them. Indeed, McCormick was
as able in business as in mechanical invention. Two
years after Ogden paid him $25,000 for a half interest
in the business, McCormick bought it back for $50,-
000; and thereafter, until his death in 1884, no one but
members of the McCormick family had any interest
in the business.

THE BANKER ERA

It may be urged that railroads and steamships, the
telegraph and harvesting machinery were introduced
before the accumulation of investment capital had developed the investment banker, and before America's
"great banking houses" had been established; and that,
consequently, it would be fairer to inquire what services bankers had rendered in connection with later industrial development. The firm of J. P. Morgan & Co.
is fifty-five years old; Kuhn, Loeb & Co. fifty-six years
old; Lee, Higginson & Co. over fifty years; and Kidder, Peabody & Co. forty-eight years; and yet the investment banker seems to have had almost as little part
in "initiating" the great improvements of the last half
century, as did bankers in the earlier period.

STEEL

The modern steel industry of America is forty-five
years old. The "great bankers" had no part in initiating it. Andrew Carnegie, then already a man of large
means, introduced the Bessemer process in 1868. In
the next thirty years our steel and iron industry increased greatly. By 1898 we had far outstripped all
competitors. America's production about equalled the
aggregate of England and Germany. We had also re-

duced costs so much that Europe talked of the "American Peril." It was 1898, when J. P. Morgan & Co. took their first step in forming the Steel Trust, by organizing the Federal Steel Company. Then followed the combination of the tube mills into an $80,000,000 corporation, J. P. Morgan & Co. taking for their syndicate services $20,000,000 of common stock. About the same time the consolidation of the bridge and structural works, the tin plate, the sheet steel, the hoop and other mills followed; and finally, in 1901, the Steel Trust was formed, with a capitalization of $1,402,000,-000. These combinations came thirty years after the steel industry had been "initiated".

THE TELEPHONE

The telephone industry is less than forty years old. It is probably America's greatest contribution to industrial development. The bankers had no part in "initiating" it. The glory belongs to a simple, enthusiastic, warm-hearted, business man of Haverhill, Massachusetts, who was willing to risk *his own* money. H. N. Casson tells of this, most interestingly, in his "History of the Telephone":

"The only man who had money and dared to stake it on the future of the telephone was Thomas Sanders, and he did this not mainly for business reasons. Both he and Hubbard were attached to Bell primarily by sentiment, as Bell had removed the blight of dumbness from Sanders' little son, and was soon to marry Hubbard's daughter. Also, Sanders had no expectation, at first, that so much money would be needed. He was not rich. His entire business, which was that of cutting out soles for shoe manufacturers, was not at any time worth more than thirty-five thousand dollars. Yet,

from 1874 to 1878, he had advanced nine-tenths of the
money that was spent on the telephone. The first five
thousand telephones, and more, were made with his
money. And so many long, expensive months dragged
by before any relief came to Sanders, that he was
compelled, much against his will and his business judgment, to stretch his credit within an inch of the break-
ing-point to help Bell and the telephone. Desperately
he signed note after note until he faced a total of one
hundred and ten thousand dollars. If the new 'scientific toy' succeeded, which he often doubted, he would
be the richest citizen in Haverhill; and if it failed,
which he sorely feared, he would be a bankrupt. Sanders and Hubbard were leasing telephones two by two,
to business men who previously had been using the
private lines of the Western Union Telegraph Company. This great corporation was at this time their
natural and inevitable enemy. It had swallowed most
of its competitors, and was reaching out to monopolize
all methods of communication by wire. The rosiest
hope that shone in front of Sanders and Hubbard was
that the Western Union might conclude to buy the
Bell patents, just as it had already bought many others.
In one moment of discouragement they had offered
the telephone to President Orton, of the Western
Union, for $100,000; and Orton had refused it. 'What
use,' he asked pleasantly, 'could this company make of
an electrical toy?'

"But besides the operation of its own wires, the
Western Union was supplying customers with various
kinds of printing-telegraphs and dial-telegraphs, some
of which could transmit sixty words a minute. These
accurate instruments, it believed, could never be dis-
placed by such a scientific oddity as the telephone, and
it continued to believe this until one of its subsidiary

companies—the Gold and Stock—reported that several of its machines had been superseded by telephones.

"At once the Western Union awoke from its indifference. Even this tiny nibbling at its business must be stopped. It took action quickly, and organized the 'American Speaking-Telephone Company,' and with $300,000 capital, and with three electrical inventors, Edison, Gray, and Dolbear, on its staff. With all the bulk of its great wealth and prestige, it swept down upon Bell and his little body-guard. It trampled upon Bell's patent with as little concern as an elephant can have when he tramples upon an ant's nest. To the complete bewilderment of Bell, it coolly announced that it had the only original telephone, and that it was ready to supply superior telephones with all the latest improvements made by the original inventors—Dolbear, Gray, and Edison.

"The result was strange and unexpected. The Bell group, instead of being driven from the field, were at once lifted to a higher level in the business world. And the Western Union, in the endeavor to protect its private lines, became involuntarily a 'bell-wether' to lead capitalists in the direction of the telephone."

Even then, when financial aid came to the Bell enterprise, it was from capitalists, not from bankers, and among these capitalists was William H. Forbes (son of the builder of the Burlington) who became the first President of the Bell Telephone Company. That was in 1878. More than twenty years later, after the telephone had spread over the world, the great house of Morgan came into financial control of the property. The American Telephone & Telegraph Company was formed. The process of combination became active. Since January, 1900, its stock has increased from $25,-886,300 to $344,606,400. In six years (1906 to 1912) the Morgan associates marketed about $300,000,000 bonds of that company or its subsidiaries. In that period the volume of business done by the telephone companies had, of course, grown greatly, and the plant had to be constantly increased; but the proceeds of these huge security issues were used, to a large extent, in effecting combinations; that is, in buying out telephone competitors; in buying control of the Western Union Telegraph Company; and in buying up outstanding stock interests in semi-independent Bell companies. It is these combinations which have led to the investigation of the Telephone Company by the Department of Justice; and they are, in large part, responsible for the movement to have the government take over the telephone business.

ELECTRICAL MACHINERY

The business of manufacturing electrical machinery and apparatus is only a little over thirty years old. J. P. Morgan & Co. became interested early in one branch of it; but their dominance of the business today is due, not to their "initiating" it, but to their effecting a combination, and organizing the General Electric Company in 1892. There were then three large electrical companies, the Thomson-Houston, the Edison and the Westinghouse, besides some small ones. The Thomson-Houston of Lynn, Massachusetts, was in many respects the leader, having been formed to introduce, among other things, important inventions of Prof. Elihu Thomson and Prof. Houston. Lynn is one of the principal shoe-manufacturing centers of America. It is within ten miles of State Street, Boston; but Thomson's early financial support came not from Boston bankers, but mainly from Lynn busi-

ness men and investors; men active, energetic, and
used to taking risks with *their own* money. Prominent
among them was Charles A. Coffin, a shoe manufacturer, who became connected with the Thomson-Houston Company upon its organization and president of
the General Electric when Mr. Morgan formed that
company in 1892, by combining the Thomson-Houston
and the Edison. To his continued service, supported
by other Thomson-Houston men in high positions, the
great prosperity of the company is, in large part, due.
The two companies so combined controlled probably
one-half of all electrical patents then existing in America; and certainly more than half of those which had
any considerable value.

In 1896 the General Electric pooled its patents with
the Westinghouse, and thus competition was further
restricted. In 1903 the General Electric absorbed the
Stanley Electric Company, its other large competitor;
and became the largest manufacturer of electric apparatus and machinery in the world. In 1912 the resources of the Company were $131,942,144. It billed
sales to the amount of $89,182,185. It employed di-
rectly over 60,000 persons,—more than a fourth as
many as the Steel Trust. And it is protected against
"undue" competition; for one of the Morgan partners
has been a director, since 1909, in the Westinghouse,—
the only other large electrical machinery company in
America.

THE AUTOMOBILE

The automobile industry is about twenty years old.
It is now America's most prosperous business. When
Henry B. Joy, President of the Packard Motor Car
Company, was asked to what extent the bankers aided
in "initiating" the automobile, he replied:

"It is the observable facts of history, it is also my experience of thirty years as a business man, banker, etc., that first the seer conceives an opportunity. He has faith in his almost second sight. He believes he can do something—develop a business—construct an industry—build a railroad—or Niagara Falls Power Company,—and make it pay!

"Now the human measure is not the actual physical construction, but the 'make it pay'!

"A man raised the money in the late '90s and built a beet sugar factory in Michigan. Wiseacres said it was nonsense. He gathered together the money from his friends who would take a chance with him. He not only built the sugar factory (and there was never any doubt of his ability to do that) but he made it pay. The next year two more sugar factories were built, and were financially successful. These were built by private individuals of wealth, taking chances in the face of cries of doubting bankers and trust companies.

"Once demonstrated that the industry was a sound one financially and *then* bankers and trust companies would lend the new sugar companies which were speedily organized a large part of the necessary funds to construct and operate.

"The motor-car business was the same.

"When a few gentlemen followed me in my vision of the possibilities of the business, the banks and older business men (who in the main were the banks) said, 'fools and their money soon to be parted'—etc., etc.

"Private capital at first establishes an industry, backs it through its troubles, and, if possible, wins financial success when banks would not lend a dollar of aid.

"The business once having proved to be practicable and financially successful, then do the banks lend aid to its needs."

Such also was the experience of the greatest of the many financial successes in the automobile industry—the Ford Motor Company.

HOW BANKERS ARREST DEVELOPMENT

But "great banking houses" have not merely failed to initiate industrial development; they have definitely arrested development because to them the creation of the trusts is largely due. The recital in the Memorial addressed to the President by the Investors' Guild in November, 1911, is significant:

"It is a well-known fact that modern trade combinations tend strongly toward constancy of process and products, and by their very nature are opposed to new processes and new products originated by independent inventors, and hence tend to restrain competition in the development and sale of patents and patent rights; and consequently tend to discourage independent inventive thought, to the great detriment of the nation, and with injustice to inventors whom the Constitution especially intended to encourage and protect in their rights."

And more specific was the testimony of the *Engineering News;*

"We are today something like five years behind Germany in iron and steel metallurgy, and such innovations as are being introduced by our iron and steel manufacturers are most of them merely following the lead set by foreigners years ago.

"We do not believe this is because American engineers are any less ingenious or originial than those of Europe, though they may indeed be deficient in training and scientific education compared with those of Germany. We believe the main cause is the wholesale consolidation which has taken place in American industry. A huge organization is too clumsy to take up the development of an original idea. With the market closely controlled and profits certain by following standard methods, those who control our trusts do not want the bother of developing anything new.

"We instance metallurgy only by way of illustration. There are plenty of other fields of industry where exactly the same condition exists. We are building the same machines and using the same methods as a dozen years ago, and the real advances in the art are being made by European inventors and manufacturers."

To which President Wilson's statement may be added:

"I am not saying that all invention had been stopped by the growth of trusts, but I think it is perfectly clear that invention in many fields has been discouraged, that inventors have been prevented from reaping the full fruits of their ingenuity and industry, and that mankind has been deprived of many comforts and conveniences, as well as the opportunity of buying at lower prices.

"Do you know, have you had occasion to learn, that there is no hospitality for invention, now-a-days?"

TRUSTS AND FINANCIAL CONCENTRATION

The fact that industrial monopolies arrest development is more serious even than the direct burden imposed through extortionate prices. But the most harmbearing incident of the trusts is their promotion of financial concentration. Industrial trusts feed the money trust. Practically every trust created has destroyed the financial independence of some communities and of many properties; for it has centered the financing of a large part of whole lines of business in New York, and this usually with one of a few banking houses. This is well illustrated by the Steel Trust, which is a trust of trusts; that is, the Steel Trust combines in one huge holding company the trusts previously formed in the different branches of the steel business. Thus the Tube Trust combined 17 tube mills, located in 16 different cities, scattered over 5 states and owned by 13 different companies. The wire trust combined 19 mills; the sheet steel trust 26; the bridge and structural trust 27; and the tin plate trust 36; all scattered similarly over many states. Finally these and other companies were formed into the United States Steel Corporation, combining 228 companies in all, located in 127 cities and towns, scattered over 18 states. Before the combinations were effected, nearly every one of these companies was owned largely by those who managed it, and had been financed, to a large extent, in the place, or in the state, in which it was located. When the Steel Trust was formed all these concerns came under one management. Thereafter, the financing of each of these 228 corporations (and some which were later acquired) had to be done through or with the consent of J. P. Morgan & Co. *That was the greatest step in financial concentration ever taken.*

STOCK EXCHANGE INCIDENTS

The organization of trusts has served in another way to increase the power of the Money Trust. Few of the independent concerns out of which the trusts have been formed, were listed on the New York Stock Exchange; and few of them had financial offices in New York. Promoters of large corporations, whose stock is to be held by the public, and also investors, desire to have their securities listed on the New York

Stock Exchange. Under the rules of the Exchange, no security can be so listed unless the corporation has a transfer agent and registrar in New York City. Furthermore, banker-directorships have contributed largely to the establishment of the financial offices of the trusts in New York City. That alone would tend to financial concentration. But the listing of the stock enhances the power of the Money Trust in another way. An industrial stock, once listed, frequently becomes the subject of active speculation; and speculation feeds the Money Trust indirectly in many ways. It draws the money of the country to New York. The New York bankers handle the loans of other people's money on the Stock Exchange; and members of the Stock Exchange receive large amounts from commissions. For instance: There are 5,084,952 shares of United States Steel common stock outstanding. But in the five years ending December 31, 1912, speculation in that stock was so extensive that there were sold on the Exchange an average of 29,380,888 shares a year; or nearly six times as much as there is Steel common in existence. Except where the transactions are by or for the brokers, sales on the Exchange involve the payment of twenty-five cents in commission for each share of stock sold; that is, twelve and one-half cents by the seller and twelve and one-half cents by the buyer. Thus the commission from the Steel common alone afforded a revenue averaging many millions a year. The Steel preferred stock is also much traded in; and there are 138 other industrials, largely trusts, listed on the New York Stock Exchange.

TRUST RAMIFICATIONS

But the potency of trusts as a factor in financial concentration is manifested in still other ways; notably through their ramifying operations. This is illustrated forcibly by the General Electric Company's control of water-power companies which has now been disclosed in an able report of the United States Bureau of Corporations:

"The extent of the General Electric influence is not fully revealed by its consolidated balance sheet. A very large number of corporations are connected with it through its subsidiaries and through corporations controlled by these subsidiaries or affiliated with them. There is a still wider circle of influence due to the fact that officers and directors of the General Electric Co. and its subsidiaries are also officers or directors of many other corporations, some of whose securities are owned by the General Electric Company.

"The General Electric Company holds in the first place all the common stock in three security holding companies: the United Electric Securities Co., the Electrical Securities Corporation, and the Electric Bond and Share Co. Directly and through these corporations and their officers the General Electric controls a large part of the water power of the United States.

. . . "The water-power companies in the General Electric group are found in 18 States. These 18 States have 2,325,757 commercial horsepower developed or under construction, and of this total the General Electric group includes 939,115 h. p. or 40.4 per cent. The greatest amount of power controlled by the companies in the General Electric group in any State is found in Washington. This is followed by New York, Pennsylvania, California, Montana, Iowa, Oregon, and Colorado. In five of the States shown in the table the water-power companies included in the General Electric group control more than 50 per cent. of the commercial power, developed and under construction. The percentage of power in the States included in the General Electric group ranges from a little less than 2 per cent. in Michigan to nearly 80 per cent. in Pennsylvania. In Colorado they control 72 per cent.; in New Hampshire 61 per cent.; in Oregon 58 per cent.; and in Washington 55 per cent.

Besides the power developed and under construction water-power concerns included in the General Electric group own in the States shown in the table 641,600 h. p. undeveloped."

This water power control enables the General Electric group to control other public service corporations:

"The water-power companies subject to General Electric influence control the street railways in at least 16 cities and towns; the electric-light plants in 78 cities and towns; gas plants in 19 cities and towns; and are affiliated with the electric light and gas plants in other towns. Though many of these communities, particularly those served with light only, are small, several of them are the most important in the States where these water-power companies operate. The water-power companies in the General Electric group own, control, or are closely affiliated with, the street railways in Portland and Salem, Ore.; Spokane, Wash.; Great Falls, Mont.; St. Louis, Mo.; Winona, Minn.; Milwaukee and Racine, Wis.; Elmira, N. Y.; Asheville and Raleigh, N. C., and other relatively less important towns. The towns in which the lighting plants (electric or gas) are owned or controlled include Portland, Salem, Astoria, and other towns in Oregon; Bellingham and other towns in Washington; Butte, Great Falls, Bozeman and other towns in Montana; Leadville and Colorado Springs in Colorado; St. Louis, Mo.; Milwaukee, Racine and several small towns in Wisconsin; Hudson and Rensselaer, N. Y.;

Detroit, Mich.; Asheville and Raleigh, N. C.; and in fact one or more towns in practically every community where developed water power is controlled by this group. In addition to the public-service corporations thus controlled by the water-power companies subject to General Electric influence, there are numerous public-service corporations in other municipalities that purchase power from the hydroelectric developments controlled by or affiliated with the General Electric Co. This is true of Denver, Colo., which has already been discussed. In Baltimore, Md., a water-power concern in the General Electric group, namely, the Pennsylvania Water & Power Co., sells 20,000 h. p. to the Consolidated Gas, Electric Light & Power Co., which controls the entire light and power business of that city. The power to operate all the electric street railway systems of Buffalo, N. Y., and vicinity, involving a trackage of approximately 375 miles, is supplied through a subsidiary of the Niagara Falls Power Co."

And the General Electric Company, through the financing of public service companies, exercises a like influence in communities where there is no water power

"It, or its subsidiaries, has acquired control of or an interest in the public-service corporations of numerous cities where there is no water-power connection, and it is affiliated with still others by virtue of common directors. . . . This vast network of relationship between hydro-electric corporations through prominent officers and directors of the largest manufacturer of electrical machinery and supplies in the United States is highly significant. . . .

"It is possible that this relationship to such a large number of strong financial concerns, through common officers and directors, affords the General Electric Co.

an advantage that may place rivals at a corresponding disadvantage. Whether or not this great financial power has been used to the particular disadvantage of any rival waterpower concern is not so important as the fact that such power exists and that it might be so used at any time."

THE SHERMAN LAW

The Money Trust cannot be broken, if we allow its power to be constantly augmented. To break the Money Trust, we must stop that power at its source. The industrial trusts are among its most effective feeders. Those which are illegal should be dissolved. The creation of new ones should be prevented. To this end the Sherman Law should be supplemented both by providing more efficient judicial machinery, and by creating a commission with administrative functions to aid in enforcing the law. When that is done, another step will have been taken toward securing the New Freedom. But restrictive legislation alone will not suffice. We should bear in mind the admonition with which the Commissioner of Corporations closes his review of our water power development:

"There is . . . presented such a situation in water powers and other public utilities as might bring about at any time under a single management the control of a majority of the developed water power in the United States and similar control over the public utilities in a vast number of cities and towns, including some of the most important in the country."

We should conserve all rights which the Federal Government and the States now have in our natural resources, and there should be a complete separation of our industries from railroads and public utilities.

CHAPTER VIII

A CURSE OF BIGNESS

Bigness has been an important factor in the rise of the Money Trust: Big railroad systems, Big industrial trusts, big public service companies; and as instruments of these Big banks and Big trust companies. J. P. Morgan & Co. (in their letter of defence to the Pujo Committee) urge the needs of Big Business as the justification for financial concentration. They declare that what they euphemistically call "coöperation" is "simply a further result of the necessity for handling great transactions"; that "the country obviously requires not only the larger individual banks, but demands also that those banks shall coöperate to perform efficiently the country's business"; and that "a step backward along this line would mean a halt in industrial progress that would affect every wage-earner from the Atlantic to the Pacific." The phrase "great transactions" is used by the bankers apparently as meaning large corporate security issues.

Leading bankers have undoubtedly coöperated during the last 15 years in floating some very large security issues, as well as many small ones. But relatively few large issues were made necessary by great improvements undertaken or by industrial development. Improvements and development ordinarily proceed slowly. For them, even where the enterprise involves large expenditures, a series of smaller issues is usually more appropriate than single large ones. This is particularly true in the East where the building of new railroads has practically ceased. The "great" security issues in which bankers have coöperated were, with relatively few exceptions, made either for the purpose of effecting combinations or as a consequence of such combinations. Furthermore, the combinations which made necessary these large security issues or underwritings were, in most cases, either contrary to existing statute law, or contrary to laws recommended by the Interstate Commerce Commission, or contrary to the laws of business efficiency. So both the financial concentration and the combinations which they have served were, in the main, against the public interest. Size, we are told, is not a crime. But size may, at least, become noxious by reason of the means through which it was attained or the uses to which it is put. And it is size attained by combination, instead of natural growth, which has contributed so largely to our financial concentration. Let us examine a few cases:

THE HARRIMAN PACIFICS

J. P. Morgan & Co., in urging the "need of large banks and the coöperation of bankers," said:

"The Attorney-General's recent approval of the Union Pacific settlement calls for a single commitment on the part of bankers of $126,000,000."

This $126,000,000 "commitment" was not made to enable the Union Pacific to secure capital. On the contrary it was a guaranty that it would succeed in disposing of its Southern Pacific stock to that amount. And when it had disposed of that stock, it was confronted with the serious problem—what to do with the proceeds? This huge underwriting became necessary solely because the Union Pacific had violated the Sherman Law. It had acquired that amount of Southern Pacific stock illegally; and the Supreme Court of the United States finally decreed that the illegality cease.

This same illegal purchase had been the occasion, twelve years earlier, of another "great transaction,"—the issue of a $100,000,000 of Union Pacific bonds, which were sold to provide funds for acquiring this Southern Pacific and other stocks in violation of law. Bankers "coöperated" also to accomplish that.

UNION PACIFIC IMPROVEMENTS

The Union Pacific and its auxiliary lines (the Oregon Short Line, the Oregon Railway and Navigation and the Oregon-Washington Railroad) made, in the fourteen years, ending June 30, 1912, issues of securities aggregating $375,158,183 (of which $46,500,000 were refunded or redeemed); but the large security issues served mainly to supply funds for engaging in illegal combinations or stock speculation. The extraordinary improvements and additions that raised the Union Pacific Railroad to a high state of efficiency were provided mainly by the net earnings from the operation of its railroads. And note how great the improvements and additions were: Tracks were straightened, grades were lowered, bridges were rebuilt, heavy rails were laid, old equipment was replaced by new; and the cost of these was charged largely as operating expense. Additional equipment was added, new lines were built or acquired, increasing the system by 3524 miles of line, and still other improvements and betterments were made and charged to capital account. These expenditures aggregated $191,512,328. But it needed no "large security issues" to provide the capital thus wisely expended. The net earnings from the operations of these railroads were so large that nearly all these improvements and additions could have been made without issuing on the average more than $1,000,000 a year of additional securities for "new money," and the company still could have paid six per cent. dividends after 1906 (when that rate was adopted). For while $13,-679,452 a year, on the average, was charged to Cost of Road and Equipment, the surplus net earnings and other funds would have yielded, on the average, $12,-750,982 a year available for improvements and additions, without raising money on new security issues.

HOW THE SECURITY PROCEEDS WERE SPENT

The $375,000,000 securities (except to the extent of about $13,000,000 required for improvements, and the amounts applied for refunding and redemptions) were available to buy stocks and bonds of other companies. And some of the stocks so acquired were sold at large profits, providing further sums to be employed in stock purchases.

The $375,000,000 Union Pacific Lines security issues, therefore, were not needed to supply funds for Union Pacific improvements; nor did these issues supply funds for the improvement of any of the companies in which the Union Pacific invested (except that certain amounts were advanced later to aid in financing the Southern Pacific). *They served, substantially, no purpose save to transfer the ownership of railroad stocks from one set of persons to another.*

Here are some of the principal investments:

1. $91,657,500, in acquiring and financing the Southern Pacific.
2. $89,391,401, in acquiring the Northern Pacific stock and stock of the Northern Securities Co.
3. $45,466,960, in acquiring Baltimore & Ohio stock.
4. $37,692,256, in acquiring Illinois Central stock.
5. $23,205,679, in acquiring New York Central stock.
6. $10,395,000, in acquiring Atchison, Topeka & Santa Fe stock.
7. $8,946,781, in acquiring Chicago & Alton stock.

8. $11,610,187, in acquiring Chicago, Milwaukee & St. Paul stock.
9. $6,750,423, in acquiring Chicago & Northwestern stock.
10. $6,936,696, in acquiring Railroad Securities Co. stock (Illinois Central stock).

The immediate effect of these stock acquisitions, as stated by the Interstate Commerce Commission in 1907, was merely this:

"Mr. Harriman may journey by steamship from New York to New Orleans, thence by rail to San Francisco, across the Pacific Ocean to China, and, returning by another route to the United States, may go to Ogden by any one of three rail lines, and thence to Kansas City or Omaha, without leaving the deck or platform of a carrier which he controls, and without duplicating any part of his journey.

"He has further what appears to be a dominant control in the Illinois Central Railroad running directly north from the Gulf of Mexico to the Great Lakes, parallel to the Mississippi River; and two thousand miles west of the Mississippi River he controls the only line of railroad parallel to the Pacific Coast, and running from the Colorado River to the Mexican border. . . .

"The testimony taken at this hearing shows that about fifty thousand square miles of territory in the State of Oregon, surrounded by the lines of the Oregon Short Line Railroad Company, the Oregon Railroad and Navigation Company, and the Southern Pacific Company, is not developed. While the funds of those companies which could be used for that purpose are being invested in stocks like the New York Central and other lines having only a remote relation to the territory in which the Union Pacific System is located."

Mr. Harriman succeeded in becoming director in 27 railroads with 39,354 miles of line; and they extended from the Atlantic to the Pacific; from the Great Lakes to the Gulf of Mexico.

THE AFTERMATH

On September 9, 1909, less than twelve years after Mr. Harriman first became a director in the Union Pacific, he died from overwork at the age of 61. But it was not death only that had set a limit to his achievements. The multiplicity of his interests prevented him from performing for his other railroads the great services that had won him a world-wide reputation as manager and rehabilitator of the Union Pacific and the Southern Pacific. Within a few months after Mr. Harriman's death the serious equipment scandal on the Illinois Central became public, culminating in the probable suicide of one of the vice-presidents of that company. The Chicago & Alton (in the management of which Mr. Harriman was prominent from 1899 to 1907, as President, Chairman of the Board, or Executive Committeeman), has never regained the prosperity it enjoyed before he and his associates acquired control. The Père Marquette has passed again into receiver's hands. Long before Mr. Harriman's death the Union Pacific had disposed of its Northern Pacific stock, because the Supreme Court of the United States declared the Northern Securities Company illegal, and dissolved the Northern Pacific-Great Northern merger. Three years after his death, the Supreme Court of the United States ordered the Union Pacific-Southern Pacific merger dissolved. By a strange irony, the law has permitted the Union Pacific to reap large profits from its illegal transactions in Northern Pacific and Southern Pacific stocks. But many other stocks held "as investments" have entailed large losses. Stocks in the Illinois Central and other companies which cost the Union Pacific $129,894,991.72, had on November 15, 1913, a market value of only $87,851,500; showing a shrinkage of $42,043,491.72 and the average income from them, while held, was only about 4.30 per cent. on their cost.

A BANKER'S PARADISE

Kuhn, Loeb & Co. were the Union Pacific bankers. It was in pursuance of a promise which Mr. Jacob H. Schiff—the senior partner—had given, pending the reorganization, that Mr. Harriman first became a member of the Executive Committee in 1897. Thereafter combinations grew and crumbled, and there were vicissitudes in stock speculations. But the investment bankers prospered amazingly; and financial concentration proceeded without abatement. The bankers and their associates received the commissions paid for purchasing the stocks which the Supreme Court holds to have been acquired illegally—and have retained them. The bankers received commissions for underwriting the securities issued to raise the money with which to buy the stocks which the Supreme Court holds to have been illegally acquired, and have retained them. The bankers received commissions paid for floating securities of the controlled companies—while they were thus controlled in violation of law—and have, of course, retained them. Finally when, after years, a decree is entered to end the illegal combination, these same bankers are on hand to perform the services of undertaker —and receive further commissions for their banker-aid in enabling the law-breaking corporation to end its wrong doing and to comply with the decree of the Supreme Court. And yet, throughout nearly all this long period, both before and after Mr. Harriman's death, two partners in Kuhn, Loeb & Co. were directors or members of the executive committee of the Union Pacific; and as such must be deemed responsible with others for the illegal acts.

Indeed, these bankers have not only received commissions for the underwritings of transactions accomplished, though illegal; they have received commissions also for merely *agreeing* to underwrite a "great transaction" which the authorities would not permit to be *accomplished*. The $126,000,000 underwriting (that "single commitment on the part of the bankers" to which J. P. Morgan & Co. refer as being called for by "the Attorney General's approval of the Union Pacific settlement") never became effective; because the Public Service Commission of California refused to approve the terms of settlement. But the Union Pacific, nevertheless, paid the Kuhn Loeb Syndicate a large underwriting fee for having been ready and willing "to serve" should the opportunity arise: and another underwriting commission was paid when the Southern Pacific stock was finally distributed, with the approval of Attorney General McReynolds, under the Court's [11] decree. Thus the illegal purchase of Southern Pacific stock yielded directly four crops of commissions; two when it was acquired, and two when it was disposed of. And during the intervening period the illegally controlled Southern Pacific yielded many more commissions to the bankers. For the schedules filed with the Pujo Committee show that Kuhn, Loeb & Co. marketed, in addition to the Union Pacific securities above referred to, $334,000,000 of Southern Pacific and Central Pacific securities between 1903 and 1911.

[11] James C. McReynolds, appointed Attorney General and later a Justice of the Supreme Court by Woodrow Wilson.

The aggregate amount of the commissions paid to these bankers in connection with Union Pacific-Southern Pacific transactions is not disclosed. It must have been very large; for not only were the transactions "great"; but the commissions were liberal. The Interstate Commerce Commission finds that bankers received about 5 per cent. on the purchase price for buying the first 750,000 shares of Southern Pacific stock; and the underwriting commission on the first $100,-000,000 Union Pacific bonds issued to make that and other purchases was $5,000,000. How large the two underwriting commissions were which the Union Pacific paid in effecting the severance of this illegal merger, both the company and the bankers have declined to disclose. Furthermore the Interstate Commerce Commission showed, clearly, while investigating the Union Pacific's purchase of the Chicago & Alton stock, that the bankers' profits were by no means confined to commissions.

THE BURLINGTON

Such railroad combinations produce injury to the public far more serious than the heavy tax of bankers' commissions and profits. For in nearly every case the absorption into a great system of a theretofore independent railroad has involved the loss of financial independence to some community, property or men, who thereby become subjects or satellites of the Money Trust. The passing of the Chicago, Burlington & Quincy, in 1901, to the Morgan associates, presents a striking example of this process.

After the Union Pacific acquired the Southern Pacific stock in 1901, it sought control, also, of the Chicago, Burlington & Quincy,—a most prosperous railroad, having then 7912 miles of line. The Great Northern and Northern Pacific recognized that Union Pacific control of the Burlington would exclude them from much of Illinois, Missouri, Wisconsin, Kansas, Nebraska, Iowa, and South Dakota. The two northern roads, which were already closely allied with each other and with J. P. Morgan & Co., thereupon purchased for $215,227,000, of their joint 4 per cent. bonds, nearly all of the $109,324,000 (par value) outstanding Burlington stock. A struggle with the Union Pacific ensued which yielded soon to "harmonious coöperation." The Northern Securities Company was formed with $400,000,000 capital, thereby merging the Great Northern, the Northern Pacific and the Burlington, and joining the Harriman, Kuhn-Loeb, with the Morgan-Hill interests. Obviously neither the issue of $215,000,000 joint 4's, nor the issue of the $400,000,000 Northern Securities stock supplied one dollar of funds for improvements of, or additions to, any of the four great railroad systems concerned in these "large transactions." *The sole effect of issuing $615,000,000 of securities was to transfer stock from one set of persons to another.* And the resulting "harmonious cooperation" was soon interrupted by the government proceedings, which ended with the dissolution of the Northern Securities Company. But the evil done outlived the combination. The Burlington had passed forever from its independent Boston owners to the Morgan allies, who remain in control.

The Burlington—one of Boston's finest achievements—was the creation of John M. Forbes. He was [12] a builder; not a combiner, or banker, or wizard of finance. He was a simple, hard-working business man. He had been a merchant in China at a time when China's trade was among America's big business. He had been connected with shipping and with manufac-

[12] Brandeis' account of John Murray Forbes (1813–1898) betrays his provincial Bostonian bias. Forbes, a director of the Chicago, Burlington & Quincy Railroad from 1857 to his death, President from 1859 to 1878,

turers. He had the imagination of the great merchant;
the patience and perseverance of the great manufacturer; the courage of the sea-farer; and the broad view
of the statesman. Bold, but never reckless; scrupulously careful of other people's money, he was ready,
after due weighing of chances, to risk his own in enterprises promising success. He was in the best sense of
the term, a great adventurer. Thus equipped, Mr.
Forbes entered, in 1852, upon those railroad enterprises
which later developed into the Chicago, Burlington &
Quincy. Largely with his own money and that of
friends who confided in him, he built these railroads
and carried them through the panic of '57, when the
"great banking houses" of those days lacked courage
to assume the burdens of a struggling ill-constructed
line, staggering under financial difficulties.

Under his wise management, and that of the men
whom he trained, the little Burlington became a great
system. It was "built on honor," and managed hon-
orably. It weathered every other great financial crisis,
as it did that of 1857. It reached maturity without a
reorganization or the sacrifice of a single stockholder or
bondholder.

Investment bankers had no place on the Burlington
Board of Directors; nor had the banker-practice, of
being on both sides of a bargain. "I am unwilling,"
said Mr. Forbes, early in his career, "to run the risk
of having the imputation of buying from a company
in which I am interested." About twenty years later
he made his greatest fight to rescue the Burlington
from the control of certain contractor-directors, whom
his biographer, Mr. Pearson, describes as "persons of
integrity, who had conceived that in their twofold
capacity as contractors and directors they were fully
able to deal with themselves justly." Mr. Forbes

and Chairman of the Board thereafter, was indeed a great entrepreneur,
but in finance, not in management. Although he was (and is) regarded
as scrupulously honest, his reputation derived largely from a stubborn

thought otherwise. The stockholders, whom he had aroused, sided with him and he won.

Mr. Forbes was the pioneer among Boston railroad-builders. His example and his success inspired many others, for Boston was not lacking then in men who were builders, though some lacked his wisdom, and some his character. Her enterprise and capital constructed, in large part, the Union Pacific, the Atchison, the Mexican Central, the Wisconsin Central, and 24 other railroads in the West and South. One by one these western and southern railroads passed out of Boston control; the greater part of them into the control of the Morgan allies. Before the Burlington was surrendered, Boston had begun to lose her dominion, even, over the railroads of New England. In 1900 the Boston & Albany was leased to the New York Central, —a Morgan property; and a few years later, another Morgan railroad—the New Haven—acquired control of nearly every other transportation line in New England. Now nothing is left of Boston's railroad dominion in the West and South, except the Eastern Kentucky Railroad—a line 36 miles long; and her control of the railroads of Massachusetts is limited to the Grafton & Upton with 19 miles of line and the Boston, Revere Beach & Lynn,—a passenger road 13 miles long.

THE NEW HAVEN MONOPOLY

The rise of the New Haven Monopoly presents another striking example of combination as a developer of financial concentration; and it illustrates also the use to which "large security issues" are put.

In 1892, when Mr. Morgan entered the New Haven directorate, it was a very prosperous little railroad with capital liabilities of $25,000,000 paying 10 per cent.

Bostonian conservatism that led him to reject the newer (and suspect) forms of finance. Brandeis easily equated this with simplicity and integrity, but business historians would regard Forbes as "unprogres-

dividends, and operating 508 miles of line. By 1899 the capitalization had grown to $80,477,600, but the aggregate mileage had also grown (mainly through merger or leases of other lines) to 2017. Fourteen years later, in 1913, when Mr. Morgan died and Mr. Mellen resigned, the mileage was 1997, just 20 miles less than in 1899; but the capital liabilities had increased to $425,935,000. Of course the business of the railroad had grown largely in those fourteen years; the road-bed was improved, bridges built, additional tracks added, and much equipment purchased; and for all this, new capital was needed; and additional issues were needed, also, because the company paid out in dividends more than it earned. But of the capital increase, over $200,000,000 was expended in the acquisition of the stock or other securities of some 121 other railroads, steamships, street railway-, electric-light-, gas- and water-companies. It was these outside properties, which made necessary the much discussed $67,000,000, 6 per cent. bond issue, as well as other large and expensive security issues. For in these fourteen years the improvements on the railroad including new equipment have cost, on the overage, only $10,000,000 a year.

THE NEW HAVEN BANKERS

Few, if any, of those 121 companies which the New Haven acquired had, prior to their absorption by it, been financed by J. P. Morgan & Co. The needs of the Boston & Maine and Maine Central—the largest group —had, for generations, been met mainly through their own stockholders or through Boston banking houses. No investment banker had been a member of the Board of Directors of either of those companies. The New York, Ontario & Western—the next largest of the

sive" and perhaps even non-innovative. An "absentee owner" of western railroads, his reputation in the West was (and is) not as golden as on State Street; and having helped direct the smashing of the

acquired railroads—had been financed in New York, but by persons apparently entirely independent of the Morgan allies. The smaller Connecticut railroads, now combined in the Central New England, had been financed mainly in Connecticut, or by independent New York bankers. The financing of the street railway companies had been done largely by individual financiers, or by small and independent bankers in the states or cities where the companies operate. Some of the steamship companies had been financed by their owners, some through independent bankers. As the result of the absorption of these 121 companies into the New Haven system, the financing of all these railroads, steamship companies, street railways, and other corporations, was made tributary to J. P. Morgan & Co.; and the independent bankers were eliminated or became satellites. *And this financial concentration was proceeded with, although practically every one of these 121 companies was acquired by the New Haven in violation either of the state or federal law, or of both.* Enforcement of the Sherman Act will doubtless result in dissolving this unwieldly illegal combination.

THE COAL MONOPOLY

Proof of the "coöperation" of the anthracite railroads is furnished by the ubiquitous presence of George F. Baker on the Board of Directors of the Reading, the Jersey Central, the Lackawanna, the Lehigh, the Erie, and the New York, Susquehanna & Western railroads, which together control nearly all the unmined anthracite as well as the actual tonnage. These roads have been an important factor in the development of the Money Trust. They are charged by the Department of Justice with fundamental violations

---

great Burlington Strike of 1886, he has a reputation in the annals of labor history that is similarly poor. Brandeis' lament for the decline of Boston's dominion expressed a sentimental attachment to his adopted

both of the Sherman Law and of the Commodity clause
of the Hepburn Act, which prohibits a railroad from
carrying, in interstate trade, any commodity in which
it has an interest, direct or indirect. Nearly every large
issue of securities made in the last 14 years by any of
these railroads (except the Erie), has been in connection with some act of combination. The combination of the anthracite railroads to suppress the construction, through the Temple Iron Company, of a
competing coal road, has already been declared illegal
by the Supreme Court of the United States. And in
the bituminous coal field—the Kanawha District—the
United States Circuit Court of Appeals has recently
decreed that a similar combination by the Lake Shore,
the Chesapeake & Ohio, and the Hocking Valley, be
dissolved.

OTHER RAILROAD COMBINATIONS

The cases of the Union Pacific and of the New
Haven are typical—not exceptional. Our railroad history presents numerous instances of large security
issues made wholly or mainly to effect combinations.
Some of these combinations have been proper as a
means of securing natural feeders or extensions of
main lines. But far more of them have been dictated
by the desire to suppress active or potential competition; or by personal ambition or greed; or by the mis-
taken belief that efficiency grows with size.

Thus the monstrous combination of the Rock Island
and the St. Louis and San Francisco with over 14,000
miles of line is recognized now to have been obviously
inefficient. It was severed voluntarily; but, had it not
been, must have crumbled soon from inherent defects,
if not as a result of proceedings under the Sherman

home town. More significantly, it symbolizes his lament for an already
dying business ethic.

law. Both systems are suffering now from the effects of this unwise combination; the Frisco, itself greatly overcombined, has paid the penalty in receivership. The Rock Island—a name once expressive of railroad efficiency and stability—has, through its excessive recapitalizations and combinations, become a football of speculators, and a source of great apprehension to confiding investors. The combination of the Cincinnati, Hamilton and Dayton, and the Père Marquette led to several receiverships.

There are, of course, other combinations which have not been disastrous to the owners of the railroads. But the fact that a railroad combination has not been disastrous does not necessarily justify it. The evil of the concentration of power is obvious; and as combination necessarily involves such concentration of power, the burden of justifying a combination should be placed upon those who seek to effect it.

For instance, what public good has been subserved by allowing the Atlantic Coast Line Railroad Company to issue $50,000,000 of securities to acquire control of the Louisville & Nashville Railroad—a widely extended, self-sufficient system of 5,000 miles, which, under the wise management of President Milton H. Smith had prospered continuously for many years be- 13 fore the acquisition; and which has gross earnings nearly twice as large as those of the Atlantic Coast Line. The legality of this combination has been recently challenged by Senator Lea; and an investigation 14 by the Interstate Commerce Commission has been ordered.

THE PENNSYLVANIA

The reports from the Pennsylvania suggest the inquiry whether even this generally well-managed railroad is not suffering from excessive bigness. After

---

[13] Brandeis may have idealized Milton Smith in much the same way that he did John Murray Forbes. In the first place, Smith had always served as the agent of the Northern financiers, so that the development Brandeis refers to was not especially novel for the Southern railway

1898 it, too, bought, in large amounts, stocks in other railroads, including the Chesapeake & Ohio, the Baltimore & Ohio, and the Norfolk & Western. In 1906 it sold all its Chesapeake & Ohio stock, and a majority of its Baltimore & Ohio and Norfolk & Western holdings. Later it reversed its policy and resumed stock purchases, acquiring, among others, more Norfolk & Western and New York, New Haven & Hartford; and on Dec. 31, 1912, held securities valued at $331,-909,154.32; of which, however, a large part represents Pennsylvania System securities. These securities (mostly stocks) constitute about one-third of the total assets of the Pennsylvania Railroad. The income on these securities in 1912 averaged only 4.30 per cent. on their valuation, while the Pennsylvania paid 6 per cent. on its stock. But the cost of carrying these foreign stocks is not limited to the difference between this income and outgo. To raise money on these stocks the Pennsylvania had to issue its own securities; and there is such a thing as an over-supply even of Pennsylvania securities. Over-supply of any stock depresses market values, and increases the cost to the Pennsylvania of raising new money. Recently came the welcome announcement of the management that it will dispose of its stocks in the anthracite coal mines; and it is intimated that it will divest itself also of other holdings in companies (like the Cambria Steel Company) extraneous to the business of railroading. This policy should be extended to include the disposition also of all stock in other railroads (like the Norfolk & Western, the Southern Pacific and the New Haven) which are not a part of the Pennsylvania System.

---

system. Moreover, Smith was not a "public servant" type of entrepreneur; as he himself put it, for 38 years he ran the Louisville & Nashville Railroad on the theory that "society, as created, was for the purpose of one man's getting what the other fellow has, if he can, and keep out of the penitentiary."

RECOMMENDATIONS

Six years ago the Interstate Commerce Commission, after investigating the Union Pacific transaction above referred to, recommended legislation to remedy the evils there disclosed. Upon concluding recently its investigation of the New Haven, the Commission repeated and amplified those recommendations, saying:

"No student of the railroad problem can doubt that a most prolific source of financial disaster and complication to railroads in the past has been the desire and ability of railroad managers to engage in enterprises outside the legitimate operation of their railroads, especially by the acquisition of other railroads and their securities. The evil which results, first, to the investing public, and, finally, to the general public, cannot be corrected after the transaction has taken place; it can be easily and effectively prohibited. In our opinion the following propositions lie at the foundation of all adequate regulation of interstate railroads:

1. Every interstate railroad should be prohibited from spending money or incurring liability or acquiring property not in the operation of its railroad or in the legitimate improvement, extension, or development of that railroad.

2. No interstate railroad should be permitted to lease or purchase any other railroad, nor to acquire the stocks or securities of any other railroad, nor to guarantee the same, directly or indirectly, without the approval of the federal government.

3. No stocks or bonds should be issued by an interstate railroad except for the purposes sanctioned in the two preceding paragraphs, and none should be issued without the approval of the federal government.

[14] Luke Lea, Democratic Senator from Tennessee.

It may be unwise to attempt to specify the price at which and the manner in which railroad stocks and securities shall be disposed of; but it is easy and safe to define the purpose for which they may be issued and to confine the expenditure of the money realized to that purpose."

These recommendations are in substantial accord with those adopted by the National Association of Railway Commissioners. They should be enacted into law. And they should be supplemented by amendments of the Commodity Clause of the Hepburn Act, so that:

1. Railroads will be effectually prohibited from owning stock in corporations whose products they transport;

2. Such corporations will be prohibited from owning important stockholdings in railroads; and

3. Holding companies will be prohibited from controlling, as does the Reading, both a railroad and corporations whose commodities it transports.

If laws such as these are enacted and duly enforced, we shall be protected from a recurrence of tragedies like the New Haven, of domestic scandals like the Chicago and Alton, and of international ones like the Frisco. We shall also escape from that inefficiency which is attendant upon excessive size. But what is far more important, we shall, by such legislation, remove a potent factor in financial concentration. Decentralization will begin. The liberated smaller units will find no difficulty in financing their needs without bowing the knee to money lords. And a long step will have been taken toward attainment of the New Freedom.

CHAPTER IX

THE FAILURE OF BANKER-MANAGEMENT

THERE is not one moral, but many, to be drawn from the Decline of the New Haven and the Fall of Mellen. That history offers texts for many sermons. It illustrates the Evils of Monopoly, the Curse of Bigness, the Futility of Lying, and the Pitfalls of Law-Breaking. But perhaps the most impressive lesson that it should teach to investors is the failure of banker-management.

BANKER CONTROL

For years J. P. Morgan & Co. were the fiscal agents of the New Haven. For years Mr. Morgan was *the* director of the Company. He gave to that property probably closer personal attention than to any other of his many interests. Stockholders' meetings are rarely interesting or important; and few indeed must have been the occasions when Mr. Morgan attended any stockholders' meeting of other companies in which he was a director. But it was his habit, when in America, to be present at meetings of the New Haven. In 1907, when the policy of monopolistic expansion was first challenged, and again at the meeting in 1909 (after Massachusetts had unwisely accorded its sanction to the Boston & Maine merger), Mr. Morgan himself moved the large increases of stock which were unanimously voted. Of course, he attended the important directors' meeting. His will was law. President Mellen [15] indicated this in his statement before Interstate Commerce Commissioner Prouty, while discussing the New

---

[15] The Morgan interests took control of the New Haven Railroad in 1903, the year Charles Sanger Mellen, then President of the Northern Pacific Railroad, became President of the New Haven. Under the

York, Westchester & Boston—the railroad without a
terminal in New York, which cost the New Haven
$1,500,000 a mile to acquire, and was then costing it,
in operating deficits and interest charges, $100,000 a
month to run:

"I am in a very embarrassing position, Mr. Commissioner, regarding the New York, Westchester &
Boston. I have never been enthusiastic or at all opti-
mistic of its being a good investment for our company
in the present, or in the immediate future; but people
in whom I had greater confidence than I have in my-
self thought it was wise and desirable; I yielded my
judgment; indeed, I don't know that it would have
made much difference whether I yielded or not."

THE BANKER'S RESPONSITILITY

Bankers are credited with being a conservative force
in the community. The tradition lingers that they are
preëminently "safe and sane." And yet, the most
grievous fault of this banker-managed railroad has
been its financial recklessness—a fault that has already
brought heavy losses to many thousands of small investors throughout New England for whom bankers
are supposed to be natural guardians. In a community
where its railroad stocks have for generations been
deemed absolutely safe investments, the passing of the
New Haven and of the Boston & Maine dividends
after an unbroken dividend record of generations
comes as a disaster.

This disaster is due mainly to enterprises outside
the legitimate operation of these railroads; for no railroad company has equaled the New Haven in the
quantity and extravagance of its outside enterprises.
But it must be remembered, that neither the president

Morgan-Mellen leadership, the New Haven began absorbing all
major means of transportation in New England, including inter-
urban street railways, coastal steamship lines and, finally, in 1907,

of the New Haven nor any other railroad manager could engage in such transactions without the sanction of the Board of Directors. It is the directors, not Mr. Mellen, who should bear the responsibility.

Close scrutiny of the transactions discloses no justification. On the contrary, scrutiny serves only to make more clear the gravity of the errors committed. Not merely were recklessly extravagant acquisitions made in mad pursuit of monopoly; but the financial judgment, the financiering itself, was conspicuously bad. To pay for property several times what it is worth, to engage in grossly unwise enterprises, are errors of which no conservative directors should be found guilty; for perhaps the most important function of directors is to test the conclusions and curb by calm counsel the excessive zeal of too ambitious managers. But while we have no right to expect from bankers exceptionally good judgment in ordinary business matters; we do have a right to expect from them prudence, reasonably good financiering, and insistence upon straightforward accounting. And it is just the lack of these qualities in the New Haven management to which the severe criticism of the Interstate Commerce Commission is particularly directed.

Commissioner Prouty calls attention to the vast increase of capitalization. During the nine years beginning July 1, 1903, the capital of the New York, New Haven & Hartford Railroad Company itself increased from $93,000,000 to about $417,000,000 (excluding premiums). That fact alone would not convict the management of reckless financiering; but the fact that so little of the new capital was represented by stock might well raise a question as to its conservativeness. For the indebtedness (including guaranties) was increased over twenty times (from about

---

the extensive Boston & Maine Railroad system. In 1913, Interstate Commerce Commissioner Charles A. Prouty launched an investigation of the New Haven, based on complaints of a breakdown in the safety

$14,000,000 to $300,000,000), while the stock outstanding in the hands of the public was not doubled ($80,-000,000 to $158,000,000). Still, in these days of large things, even such growth of corporate liabilities might be consistent with "safe and sane management."

But what can be said in defense of the financial judgment of the banker-management under which these two railroads find themselves confronted, in the fateful year 1913, with a most disquieting floating indebtedness? On March 31, the New Haven had outstanding $43,000,000 in short-time notes; the Boston & Maine had then outstanding $24,500,000, which have been increased since to $27,000,000; and additional notes have been issued by several of its subsidiary lines. Mainly to meet its share of these loans, the New Haven, which before its great expansion could sell at par 3 1/2 per cent. bonds convertible into stock at $150 a share, was so eager to issue at par $67,-500,000 of its 6 per cent. 20-year bonds convertible into stock as to agree to pay J. P. Morgan & Co. a 2 1/2 per cent. underwriting commission. True, money was "tight" then. But is it not very bad financiering to be so unprepared for the "tight" money market which had been long expected? Indeed, the New Haven's management, particularly, ought to have avoided such an error; for it committed a similar one in the "tight" money maiket of 1907-1908, when it had to sell at par $39,000,000 of its 6 per cent. 40-year bonds.

These huge short-time borrowings of the System were not due to unexpected emergencies or to their monetary conditions. They were of gradual growth. On June 30, 1910, the two companies owed in short-term notes only $10,180,364; by June 30, 1911, the amount had grown to $30,759,959; by June 30, 1912, to $45,395,000; and in 1913 to over $70,000,000. Of

---

and service of the railroad. That July, shortly after the death of the elder J. P. Morgan, a stockholders' rebellion forced Mellen's resignation, and a year later the Company declared bankruptcy. In subsequent

course the rate of interest on the loans increased also very largely. And these loans were incurred unnecessarily. They represent, in the main, not improvements on the New Haven or on the Boston & Maine Railroads, but money borrowed either to pay for stocks in other companies which these companies could not afford to buy, or to pay dividends which had not been earned.

In five years out of the last six the New Haven Railroad has, on its own showing, paid dividends in excess of the year's earnings; and the annual deficits disclosed would have been much larger if proper charges for depreciation of equipment and of steamships had been made. In each of the last three years, during which the New Haven had absolute control of the Boston & Maine, the latter paid out in dividends so much in excess of earnings that before April, 1913, the surplus accumulated in earlier years had been converted into a deficit.

Surely these facts show, at least, an extraordinary lack of financial prudence.

WHY BANKER-MANAGEMENT FAILED

Now, how can the failure of the banker-management of the New Haven be explained?

A few have questioned the ability; a few the integrity of the bankers. Commissioner Prouty attributed the mistakes made to the Company's pursuit of a transportation monopoly.

"The reason," says he, "is as apparent as the fact itself. The present management of that Company started out with the purpose of controlling the transportation facilities of New England. In the accomplishment of that purpose it bought what must be had and paid what must be paid. To this purpose and its

---

Federal antitrust proceedings by the Wilson Administration, the B.&M. regained its independence but, fearful of injuring New England's commerce, the Federal government took no punitive action against

attempted execution can be traced every one of these financial misfortunes and derelictions."

But it still remains to find the cause of the bad judgment exercised by the eminent banker-manakement in entering upon and in carrying out the policy of monopoly. For there were as grave errors in the execution of the policy of monopoly as in its adoption. Indeed, it was the aggregation of important errors of detail which compelled first the reduction, then the passing of dividends and which ultimately impaired the Company's credit.

The failure of the banker-management of the New Haven cannot be explained as the shortcomings of individuals. The failure was not accidental. It was not exceptional. It was the natural result of confusing the functions of banker and business man.

UNDIVIDED LOYALTY

The banker should be detached from the business for which he performs the banking service. This detachment is desirable, in the first place, in order to avoid conflict of interest. The relation of banker-directors to corporations which they finance has been a subject of just criticism. Their conflicting interests necessarily prevent single-minded devotion to the corporation. When a banker-director of a railroad decides as railroad man that it shall issue securities, and then sells them to himself as banker, fixing the price at which they are to be taken, there is necessarily grave danger that the interests of the railroad may suffer— suffer both through issuing of securities which ought not to be issued, and from selling them at a price less favorable to the company than should have been obtained. For it is ordinarily impossible for a banker-director to judge impartially between the corporation

---

the corporation or the financial interests behind it. Mellen escaped prosecution by agreeing to testify freely in exchange for immunity, but the exposure of the man's pusillanimity in his relationship with

and himself. Even if he succeeded in being impartial, the relation would not conduce to the best interests of the company. The best bargains are made when buyer and seller are represented by different persons.

DETACHMENT AN ESSENTIAL

But the objection to banker-management does not rest wholly, or perhaps mainly, upon the importance of avoiding divided loyalty. A complete detachment of the banker from the corporation is necessary in order to secure for the railroad the benefit of the clearest financial judgment; for the banker's judgment will be necessarily clouded by participation in the management or by ultimate responsibility for the policy actually pursued. It is *outside* financial advice which the railroad needs.

Long ago it was recognized that "a man who is his own lawyer has a fool for a client." The essential reason for this is that soundness of judgment is easily obscured by self-interest. Similarly, it is not the proper function of the banker to construct, purchase, or operate railroads, or to engage in industrial enterprises. The proper function of the banker is to give to or to withhold credit from other concerns; to purchase or to refuse to purchase securities from other concerns; and to sell securities to other customers. The proper exercise of this function demands that the banker should be wholly detached from the concern whose credit or securities are under consideration. His decision to grant or to withhold credit, to purchase or not to purchase securities, involves passing judgment on the efficiency of the management or the soundness of the enterprise; and he ought not to occupy a position where in so doing he is passing judgment on him-

---

Morgan may perhaps be regarded as punishment enough for so outrageously truculent a person.

self. Of course detachment does not imply lack of knowledge. The banker should act only with full knowledge, just as a lawyer should act only with full knowledge. The banker who undertakes to make loans to or purchase securities from a railroad for sale to his other customers ought to have as full knowledge of its affairs as does its legal adviser. But the banker should not be, in any sense, his own client. He should not, in the capacity of banker, pass judgment upon the wisdom of his own plans or acts as railroad man.

Such a detached attitude on the part of the banker is demanded also in the interest of his other customers —the purchasers of corporate securities. The investment banker stands toward a large part of his customers in a position of trust, which should be fully recognized. The small investors, particularly the women, who are holding an ever-increasing proportion of our corporate securities, commonly buy on the recommendation of their bankers. The small investors do not, and in most cases cannot, ascertain for themselves the facts on which to base a proper judgment as to the soundness of securities offered. And even if these investors were furnished with the facts, they lack the business experience essential to forming a proper judgment. Such investors need and are entitled to have the bankers' advice, and obviously their unbiased advice; and the advice cannot be unbiased where the banker, as part of the corporation's management, has participated in the creation of the securities which are the subject of sale to the investor.

Is it conceivable that the great house of Morgan would have aided in providing the New Haven with the hundreds of millions so unwisely expended, if its judgment had not been clouded by participation in the New Haven's management?

CHAPTER X

THE INEFFICIENCY OF THE OLIGARCHS

We must break the Money Trust or the Money Trust will break us.

The Interstate Commerce Commission said in its report on the most disastrous of the recent wrecks on the New Haven Railroad:

"On this directorate were and are men whom the confiding public recognize as magicians in the art of finance, and wizards in the construction, operation, and consolidation of great systems of railroads. The public therefore rested secure that with the knowledge of the railroad art possessed by such men investments and travel should both be safe. Experience has shown that this reliance of the public was not justified as to either finance or safety."

This failure of banker-management is not surprising. The surprise is that men should have supposed it would succeed. For banker-management contravenes the fundamental laws of human limitations: *First,* that no man can serve two masters; *second,* that a man cannot at the same time do many things well.

SEEMING SUCCESSES

There are numerous seeming exceptions to these rules; and a relatively few real ones. Of course, many banker-managed properties have been prosperous; some for a long time, at the expense of the public; some for a shorter time, because of the impetus attained before they were banker-managed. It is not difficult to have a large net income, where one has the field to oneself, has all the advantage privilege can give, and may "charge all the traffic will bear." And even in competitive business the success of a long-established, well-organized business with a widely extended good will, must continue for a considerable time; especially if buttressed by intertwined relations constantly giving it the preference over competitors. The real test of efficiency comes when success has to be struggled for; when natural or legal conditions limit the charges which may be made for the goods sold or service rendered. Our banker-managed railroads have recently been subjected to such a test, and they have failed to pass it. "It is only," says Goethe, "when working within limitations, that the master is disclosed."

WHY OLIGARCHY FAILS

Banker-management fails, partly because the private interest destroys soundness of judgment and undermines loyalty. It fails partly, also, because banker directors are led by their occupation (and often even by the mere fact of their location remote from the operated properties) to apply a false test in making their decisions. Prominent in the banker-director mind is always this thought: "What will be the probable effect of our action upon the market value of the company's stock and bonds, or, indeed, generally upon stock exchange values?" The stock market is so much a part of the investment-banker's life, that he cannot help being affected by this consideration, however disinterested he may be. The stock market is sensitive. Facts are often misinterpreted "by the street" or by investors. And with the best of intentions, directors susceptible to such influences are led to unwise decisions in the effort to prevent misinterpretations. Thus, expenditures necessary for maintenance, or for the ultimate good of a property are often deferred by banker-directors, because of the belief that the making of them *now,* would (by showing smaller net earnings), create a bad, and even false, impression on the market. Dividends are paid which should not be, because of the effect which it is believed reduction or suspension would have upon the market value of the company's securities. To exercise a sound judgment in the difficult affairs of business is, at best, a delicate operation. And no man can successfully perform that function whose mind is diverted, however innocently, from the study of, "what is best in the long run for the company of which I am director?" The banker-director is peculiarly liable to such distortion of judgment by reason of his occupation and his environment. But there is a further reason why, ordinarily, banker-management must fail.

THE ELEMENT OF TIME

The banker, with his multiplicity of interests, cannot ordinarily give the time essential to proper supervision and to acquiring that knowledge of the facts necessary to the exercise of sound judgment. The *Century Dictionary* tells us that a Director is "one who directs; one who guides, superintends, governs and manages." Real efficiency in any business in which conditions are ever changing must ultimately depend, in large measure, upon the correctness of the judgment exercised, almost from day to day, on the important problems as they arise. And how can the leading bankers, necessarily engrossed in the problems of their own vast private business, get time to know and to correlate the facts concerning so many other complex businesses?

Besides, they start usually with ignorance of the particular business which they are supposed to direct. When the last paper was signed which created the Steel Trust, one of the lawyers (as Mr. Perkins frankly tells us) said: "That signature is the last one necessary to put the Steel industry, on a large scale, into the hands of men who do not know anything about it."

AVOCATIONS OF THE OLIGARCHS

The New Haven System is not a railroad, but an agglomeration of a railroad plus 121 separate corporations, control of which was acquired by the New Haven after that railroad attained its full growth of about 2,000 miles of line. In administering the railroad and each of the properties formerly managed through these 122 separate companies, there must arise from time to time difficult questions on which the directors should pass judgment. The real managing directors of the New Haven system during the decade of its decline were: J. Pierpont Morgan, George F. Baker, and William Rockefeller. Mr. Morgan was, until his death in 1913, the head of perhaps the largest banking house in the world. Mr. Baker was, until 1909, President and then Chairman of the Board of Directors of one of America's leading banks (the First National of New York), and Mr. Rockefeller was, until 1911, President of the Standard Oil Company. Each was well advanced in years. Yet each of these men, besides the duties of his own vast business, and important private interests, undertook to "guide, superintend, govern and manage," not only the New Haven but also the following other corporations, some of which were similarly complex: Mr. Morgan, 48 corportaions, including 40 railroad corporations, with at least 100 subsidiary companies, and 16,000 miles of line; 3 banks and trust or insurance companies; 5 industrial and public-service companies. Mr. Baker, 48 corporations, including 15 railroad corporations, with at least 158 subsidiaries, and 37,400 miles of track; 18 banks, and trust or insurance companies; 15 public-service corporations and industrial concerns. Mr. Rockefeller, 37 corporations, including 23 railroad corporations with at least 117 subsidiary companies, and 26,400 miles of line; 5 banks, trust or insurance companies; 9 public service companies and industrial concerns.

SUBSTITUTES

It has been urged that in view of the heavy burdens which the leaders of finance assume in directing Business-America, we should be patient of error and refrain from criticism, lest the leaders be deterred from continuing to perform this public service. A very respectable Boston daily said a few days after Commissioner McCord's report on the North Haven wreck: [16]
"It is believed that the New Haven pillory repeated with some frequency will make the part of railroad director quite undesirable and hard to fill, and more and more avoided by responsible men. Indeed it may even become so that men will have to be paid a substantial salary to compensate them in some degree for the risk involved in being on the board of directors."

But there is no occasion for alarm. The American people have as little need of oligarchy in business as in politics. There are thousands of men in America who could have performed for the New Haven stockholders the task of one "who guides, superintends, governs and manages," better than did Mr. Morgan, Mr. Baker and Mr. Rockefeller. For though possessing less native ability, even the average business man would have done

---

[16] Interstate Commerce Commissioner Charles C. McChord—misspelled here by Brandeis. He had served as Chairman of the Kentucky Railroad Commission before his appointment to the I.C.C. by Taft.

better than they, because working under proper conditions. There is great strength in serving with singleness of purpose one master only. There is great strength in having time to give to a business the attention which its difficult problems demand. And tens of thousands more Americans could be rendered competent to guide our important businesses. Liberty is the greatest developer. Herodotus tells us that while the tyrants ruled, the Athenians were no better fighters than their neighbors; but when freed, they immediately surpassed all others. If industrial democracy—true coöperation—should be substituted for industrial absolutism, there would be no lack of industrial leaders.

ENGLAND'S BIG BUSINESS

England, too, has big business. But her big business is the Coöperative Wholesale Society, with a wonderful story of 50 years of beneficent growth. Its annual turnover is now about $150,000,000—an amount exceeded by the sales of only a few American industrials; an amount larger than the gross receipts of any American railroad, except the Pennsylvania and the New York Central systems. Its business is very diversified, for its purpose is to supply the needs of its members. It includes that of wholesale dealer, of manufacturer, of grower, of miner, of banker, of insurer and of carrier. It operates the biggest flour mills and the biggest shoe factory in all Great Britain. It manufactures woolen cloths, all kinds of men's, women's and children's clothing, a dozen kinds of prepared foods, and as many household articles. It operates creameries. It carries on every branch of the printing business. It is now buying coal lands. It has a bacon factory in Denmark, and a tallow and oil factory in Australia. It grows tea in Ceylon. And through all the purchasing done by the Society runs this general principle: Go direct to the source of production, whether at home or abroad, so as to save commissions of middlemen and agents. Accordingly, it has buyers and warehouses in the United States, Canada, Australia, Spain, Denmark and Sweden. It owns steamers plying between Continental and English ports. It has an important banking department; it insures the property and person of its members. Every one of these departments is conducted in competition with the most efficient concerns in their respective lines in Great Britain. The Coöperative Wholesale Society makes its purchases, and manufactures its products, in order to supply the 1399 local distributive, coöperative societies scattered over all England; but each local society is at liberty to buy from the wholesale society, or not, as it chooses; and they buy only if the Coöperative Wholesale sells at market prices. This the Coöperative actually does; and it is able besides to return to the local a fair divident on its purchases.

INDUSTRIAL DEMOCRACY

Now, how are the directors of this great business chosen? Not by England's leading bankers, or other notabilities, supposed to possess unusual wisdom; but democratically, by all of the people interested in the operations of the Society. And the number of such persons who have directly or indirectly a voice in the selection of the directors of the English Coöperative Wholesale Society is 2,750,000. For the directors of the Wholesale Society are elected by vote of the delegates of the 1399 retail societies. And the delegates of the retail societies are, in turn, selected by the members of the local societies;—that is, by the consumers, on the principle of one man, one vote, regardless of the amount of capital contributed. Note what kind of ,men these industrial democrats select to exercise executive control of their vast organization. Not all-wise bankers or their dummies, but men who have risen from the ranks of coöperation; men who, by conspicuous service in the local societies have won the respect and confidence of their fellows. The directors are elected for one year only; but a director is rarely unseated. J. T. W. Mitchell was president of the Society continuously for 21 years. Thirty-two directors are selected in this manner. Each gives to the business of the Society his whole time and attention; and the aggregate salaries of the thirty-two is less than that cf many a single executive in American corporations; for these directors of England's big business serve each for a salary of about $1500 a year.

The Coöperative Wholesale Society of England is the oldest and largest of these institutions. But similar wholesale societies exist in 15 other countries. The Scotch Society (which William Maxwell has served most efficiently as President for thirty years at a salary never exceeding $38 a week) has a turn-over of more than $50,000,000 a year.

A REMEDY FOR TRUSTS

Albert Sonnichsen, General Secretary of the Coöperative League, tells in the *American Review of Reviews* for April, 1913, how the Swedish Wholesale Society curbed the Sugar Trust; how it crushed the Margerine Combine (compelling it to dissolve after having lost 2,300,000 crowns in the struggle); and how in Switzerland the Wholesale Society forced the dissolu-

tion of the Shoe Manufacturers Association. He tells also this memorable incident:
"Six years ago, at an international congress in Cremona, Dr. Hans Müller, a Swiss delegate, presented a resolution by which an international wholesale society should be created. Luigi Luzzatti, Italian Minister of State and an ardent member of the movement, was in the chair. Those who were present say Luzzatti paused, his eyes lighted up, then, dramatically raising his hand, he said: 'Dr. Müller proposes to the assembly a great idea—that of opposing to the great trusts, the Rockefellers of the world, a world-wide coöperative alliance which shall become so powerful as to crush the trusts'."

COÖPERATION IN AMERICA

America has no Wholesale Coöperative Society able to grapple with the trusts. But it has some very strong retail societies, like the Tamarack of Michigan, which has distributed in dividends to its members $1,144,000 in 23 years. The recent high cost of living has greatly stimulated interest in the coöperative movement; and John Graham Brooks reports that we have already [17] about 350 local distributive societies. The movement toward federation is progressing. There are over 100 coöperative stores in Minnesota, Wisconsin and other Northwestern states, many of which were organized by or through the zealous work of Mr. Tousley and his associates of the Right Relationship League and are in some ways affiliated. In New York City 83 organizations are affiliated with the Coöperative League. In New Jersey the societies have federated into the American Coöperative Alliance of Northern New Jersey. In California, long the seat of effective coöperative

[17] John Graham Brooks (1846–1938), sociologist and reformer, left the Unitarian ministry in 1891 to devote himself to analyzing and writing about labor-employer relationships.

work, a central management committee is developing. And progressive Wisconsin has recently legislated wisely to develop coöperation throughout the state.

Among our farmers the interest in coöperation is especially keen. The federal government has just established a separate bureau of the Department of Agriculture to aid in the study, development and introduction of the best methods of coöperation in the working of farms, in buying, and in distribution; and special attention is now being given to farm credits—a field of coöperation in which Continental Europe has
18 achieved complete success, and to which David Lubin, America's delegate to the International Institute of Agriculture at Rome, has, among others, done much to direct our attention.

PEOPLE'S SAVINGS BANKS

The German farmer has achieved democratic banking. The 13,000 little coöperative credit associations, with an average membership of about 90 persons, are truly banks of the people, by the people and for the people.

First: The banks' resources are *of* the people. These aggregate about $500,000,000. Of this amount $375,-000,000 represents the farmers' savings deposits; $50,-000,000, the farmers' current deposits; $6,000,000, the farmers' share capital; and $13,000,000, amounts earned and placed in the reserve. Thus, nearly nine-tenths of these large resources belong to the farmers—that is, to the members of the banks.

Second: The banks are managed *by* the people—that is, the members. And membership is easily attained; for the average amount of paid-up share capital was, in 1909, less than $5 per member. Each member has

---

18 David Lubin, agriculturalist and reformer, was born in Klodowa, Russian Poland, in 1849. He settled in California in 1865, where he built the largest mail-order merchandising business in the West, organized a campaign against the Southern Pacific Railroad and other

one vote regardless of the number of his shares or the amount of his deposits. These members elect the officers. The committees and trustees (and often even, the treasurer) serve without pay: so that the expenses of the banks are, on the average, about $150 a year.

Third: The banks are *for* the people. The farmers' money is loaned by the farmer to the farmer at a low rate of interest (usually 4 per cent. to 6 per cent.); the shareholders receiving, on their shares, the same rate of interest that the borrowers pay on their loans. Thus the resources of all farmers are made available to each farmer, for productive purposes.

This democratic rural banking is not confined to Germany. As Henry W. Wolff says in his book on coöperative banks:

"Propagating themselves by their own merits, little people's coöperative banks have overspread Germany, Italy, Austria, Hungary, Switzerland, Belgium. Russia is following up those countries; France is striving strenuously for the possession of coöperative credit. Servia, Roumania, and Bulgaria have made such credit their own. Canada has scored its first success on the road to its acquisition. Cyprus, and even Jamaica, have made their first start. Ireland has substantial firstfruits to show of her economic sowings.

"South Africa is groping its way to the same goal. Egypt has discovered the necessity of coöperative banks, even by the side of Lord Cromer's pet creation, the richly endowed 'agricultural bank.' India has made a beginning full of promise. And even in far Japan, and in China, people are trying to acclimatize the more perfected organizations of Schulze-Delitsch and Raffeisen. The entire world seems girdled with a ring of coöperative credit. Only the United States and Great Britain still lag lamentably behind."

---

corporations practicing discriminatory pricing of farm commodities, and eventually helped to create an international agricultural organization to bolster the farmer's trade position (it was ratified by treaty among forty-six nations in 1910). He died in Italy in 1919.

BANKERS' SAVINGS BANKS

The savings banks of America present a striking contrast to these democratic banks. Our savings banks also have performed a great service. They have provided for the people's funds safe depositories with some income return. Thereby they have encouraged thrift and have created, among other things, reserves for the proverbial "rainy day." They have also discouraged "old stocking" hoarding, which diverts the money of the country from the channels of trade. American savings banks are also, in a sense, banks *of* the people; for it is the people's money which is administered by them. The $4,500,000,000 deposits in 2,000 American savings banks belong to about ten million people, who have an average deposit of about $450. But our savings banks are not banks *by* the people, nor, in the full sense, *for* the people.

First: American savings banks are not managed *by* the people. The stock-savings banks, most prevalent in the Middle West and the South, are purely commercial enterprises, managed, of course, by the stockholders' representatives. The mutual savings banks, most prevalent in the Eastern states, have no stockholders; but the depositors have no voice in the management. The banks are managed by trustees *for* the people, practically a self-constituted and self-perpetuating body, composed of "leading" and, to a large extent, public-spirited citizens. Among them (at least in the larger cities) there is apt to be a predominance of investment bankers, and bank directors. Thus the three largest savings banks of Boston (whose aggregate deposits exceed those of the other 18 banks) have together 81 trustees. Of these, 52 are investment bankers or directors in other Massachusetts banks or trust companies.

Second: The funds of our savings banks (whether stock or purely mutual) are not used mainly *for* the people. The depositors are allowed interest (usually from 3 to 4 per cent.). In the mutual savings banks they receive ultimately all the net earnings. But the money gathered in these reservoirs is not used to aid *productively* persons of the classes who make the deposits. The depositors are largely wage earners, salaried people, or members of small tradesmen's families. Statically the money is used for them. Dynamically it is used for the capitalist. For rare, indeed, are the instances when savings banks' moneys are loaned to advance productively one of the depositor class. Such persons would seldom be able to provide the required security; and it is doubtful whether their small needs would, in any event, receive consideration. In 1912 the largest of Boston's mutual savings banks — the Provident Institution for Savings, which is the pioneer mutual savings bank of America— managed $53,000,000 of people's money. Nearly one-half of the resources ($24,262,072) was invested in bonds—state, municipal, railroad, railway and telephone and in bank stock; or was deposited in national banks or trust companies. Two-fifths of the resources ($20,764,770) were loaned on real estate mortgages; and the average amount of a loan was $52,569. One-seventh of the resources ($7,566,612) was loaned on personal security; and the average of each of these loans was $54,830. Obviously, the "small man" is not conspicuous among the borrowers; and these large-scale investments do not even serve the individual depositor especially well; for this bank pays it depositors a rate of interest lower than the average. Even our ad-

mirable Postal Savings Bank system serves productively mainly the capitalist. These postal saving stations are in effect catch-basins merely, which collect
the people's money for distribution among the national
banks.

PROGRESS

Alphonse Desjardins of Levis, Province of Quebec,
has demonstrated that coöperative credit associations
are applicable, also, to at least some urban communities. Levis, situated on the St. Lawrence opposite the
City of Quebec, is a city of 8,000 inhabitants. Desjardins himself is a man of the people. Many years
ago he became impressed with the fact that the people's savings were not utilized primarily to aid the
people productively. There were then located in Levis
branches of three ordinary banks of deposit—a mutual
savings bank, the postal savings bank, and three incorporated "loaners"; but the people were not served.
After much thinking, he chanced to read of the European rural banks. He proceeded to work out the idea
for use in Levis; and in 1900 established there the first
"credit-union." For seven years he watched carefully
the operations of this little bank. The pioneer union
had accumulated in that period $80,000 in resources.
It had made 2,900 loans to its members, aggregating
$350,000; the loans averaging $120 in amount, and the
interest rate 6 1/2 per cent. In all this time the bank
had *not met with a single loss*. Then Desjardins concluded that democratic banking was applicable to Canada; and he proceeded to establish other credit-unions.
In the last 5 years the number of credit-unions in the
Province of Quebec has grown to 121; and 19 have
been established in the Province of Ontario. Desjar-

dins was not merely the pioneer. All the later credit-unions also have been established through his aid; and 24 applications are now in hand requesting like assistance from him. Year after year that aid has been given without pay by this public-spirited man of large family and small means, who lives as simply as the ordinary mechanic. And it is noteworthy that this rapidly extending system of coöperative credit-banks has been established in Canada wholly without government aid, Desjardins having given his services free, and his travelling expenses having been paid by those seeking his assistance.

In 1909, Massachusetts, under Desjardins' guidance, enacted a law for the incorporation of credit-unions. The first union established in Springfield, in 1910, was named after Herbert Myrick—a strong advocate of coöperative finance. Since then 25 other unions have been formed; and the names of the unions and of their officers disclose that 11 are Jewish, 8 French-Canadian, and 2 Italian—a strong indication that the immigrant is not unprepared for financial democracy. There is reason to believe that these people's banks will spread rapidly in the United States and that they will succeed. For the coöperative building and loan associations, managed by wage-earners and salary-earners, who joined together for systematic saving and ownership of houses—have prospered in many states. In Massachusetts, where they have existed for 35 years, their success has been notable—the number, in 1912, being 162, and their aggregate assets nearly $75,000,-000.

Thus farmers, workingmen, and clerks are learning to use their little capital and their savings to help one another instead of turning over their money to the great bankers for safe keeping, and to be themselves exploited. And may we not expect that when the coöperative movement develops in America, merchants and manufacturers will learn from farmers and workingmen how to help themselves by helping one another, and thus join in attaining the New Freedom for all? When merchants and manufacturers learn this lesson, money kings will lose subjects, and swollen fortunes may shrink; but industries will flourish, because the faculties of men will be liberated and developed.

President Wilson has said wisely:

"No country can afford to have its prosperity originated by a small controlling class. The treasury of America does not lie in the brains of the small body of men now in control of the great enterprises. . . . It depends upon the inventions of unknown men, upon the originations of unknown men, upon the ambitions of unknown men. Every country is renewed out of the ranks of the unknown, not out of the ranks of the already famous and powerful in control."

Revised June, 1967

haRper ♦ torchbooks

HUMANITIES AND SOCIAL SCIENCES

American Studies: General

THOMAS C. COCHRAN: The Inner Revolution. *Essays on the Social Sciences in History*   TB/1140

HENRY STEELE COMMAGER, Ed.: The Struggle for Racial Equality   TB/1300

EDWARD S. CORWIN: American Constitutional History. *Essays edited by Alpheus T. Mason and Gerald Garvey* △   TB/1136

CARL N. DEGLER, Ed.: Pivotal Interpretations of American History   TB/1240, TB/1241

A. HUNTER DUPREE: Science in the Federal Government: *A History of Policies and Activities to 1940*   TB/573

A. S. EISENSTADT, Ed.: The Craft of American History: *Recent Essays in American Historical Writing*
    Vol. I   TB/1255;   Vol. II   TB/1256

CHARLOTTE P. GILMAN: Women and Economics: *A Study of the Economic Relation between Men and Women as a Factor in Social Evolution.* ‡ *Ed. with an Introduction by Carl N. Degler*   TB/3073

OSCAR HANDLIN, Ed.: This Was America: *As Recorded by European Travelers in the Eighteenth, Nineteenth and Twentieth Centuries. Illus.*   TB/1119

MARCUS LEE HANSEN: The Atlantic Migration: 1607-1860. *Edited by Arthur M. Schlesinger*   TB/1052

MARCUS LEE HANSEN: The Immigrant in American History.   TB/1120

JOHN HIGHAM, Ed.: The Reconstruction of American History △   TB/1068

ROBERT H. JACKSON: The Supreme Court in the American System of Government   TB/1106

JOHN F. KENNEDY: A Nation of Immigrants. △ *Illus.*   TB/1118

LEONARD W. LEVY, Ed.: American Constitutional Law: *Historical Essays*   TB/1285

LEONARD W. LEVY, Ed.: Judicial Review and the Supreme Court   TB/1296

LEONARD W. LEVY: The Law of the Commonwealth and Chief Justice Shaw   TB/1309

RALPH BARTON PERRY: Puritanism and Democracy   TB/1138

ARNOLD ROSE: The Negro in America   TB/3048

MAURICE R. STEIN: The Eclipse of Community. *An Interpretation of American Studies*   TB/1128

W. LLOYD WARNER and Associates: Democracy in Jonesville: *A Study in Quality and Inequality* ¶   TB/1129

W. LLOYD WARNER: Social Class in America: *The Evaluation of Status*   TB/1013

American Studies: Colonial

BERNARD BAILYN, Ed.: Apologia of Robert Keayne: *Self-Portrait of a Puritan Merchant*   TB/1201

BERNARD BAILYN: The New England Merchants in the Seventeenth Century   TB/1149

JOSEPH CHARLES: The Origins of the American Party System   TB/1049

CHARLES GIBSON: Spain in America †   TB/3077

LAWRENCE HENRY GIPSON: The Coming of the Revolution: 1763-1775. † *Illus.*   TB/3007

LEONARD W. LEVY: Freedom of Speech and Press in Early American History: *Legacy of Suppression*   TB/1109

PERRY MILLER: Errand Into the Wilderness   TB/1139

PERRY MILLER & T. H. JOHNSON, Eds.: The Puritans: *A Sourcebook of Their Writings*
    Vol. I   TB/1093;   Vol. II   TB/1094

EDMUND S. MORGAN, Ed.: The Diary of Michael Wigglesworth, 1653-1657: *The Conscience of a Puritan*   TB/1228

EDMUND S. MORGAN: The Puritan Family: *Religion and Domestic Relations in Seventeenth-Century New England*   TB/1227

RICHARD B. MORRIS: Government and Labor in Early America   TB/1244

KENNETH B. MURDOCK: Literature and Theology in Colonial New England   TB/99

WALLACE NOTESTEIN: The English People on the Eve of Colonization: 1603-1630. † *Illus.*   TB/3006

JOHN P. ROCHE: Origins of American Political Thought: *Selected Readings*   TB/1301

JOHN SMITH: Captain John Smith's America: *Selections from His Writings. Ed. with Intro. by John Lankford*   TB/3078

LOUIS B. WRIGHT: The Cultural Life of the American Colonies: 1607-1763. † *Illus.*   TB/3005

American Studies: From the Revolution to 1860

JOHN R. ALDEN: The American Revolution: 1775-1783. † *Illus.*   TB/3011

MAX BELOFF, Ed.: The Debate on the American Revolution, 1761-1783: *A Sourcebook* △   TB/1225

RAY A. BILLINGTON: The Far Western Frontier: 1830-1860. † *Illus.*   TB/3012

EDMUND BURKE: On the American Revolution: *Selected Speeches and Letters.* ‡ *Edited by Elliott Robert Barkan*   TB/3068

WHITNEY R. CROSS: The Burned-Over District: *The Social and Intellectual History of Enthusiastic Religion in Western New York, 1800-1850* △   TB/1242

GEORGE DANGERFIELD: The Awakening of American Nationalism: 1815-1828. † *Illus.*   TB/3061

CLEMENT EATON: The Freedom-of-Thought Struggle in the Old South. *Revised and Enlarged. Illus.*   TB/1150

CLEMENT EATON: The Growth of Southern Civilization: 1790-1860. † *Illus.*   TB/3040

---

† The New American Nation Series, edited by Henry Steele Commager and Richard B. Morris.
‡ American Perspectives series, edited by Bernard Wishy and William E. Leuchtenburg.
* The Rise of Modern Europe series, edited by William L. Langer.
** History of Europe series, edited by J. H. Plumb.
¶ Researches in the Social, Cultural and Behavioral Sciences, edited by Benjamin Nelson.
§ The Library of Religion and Culture, edited by Benjamin Nelson.
Σ Harper Modern Science Series, edited by James R. Newman.
° Not for sale in Canada.
△ Not for sale in the U. K.

LOUIS FILLER: The Crusade Against Slavery: 1830-1860. †
Illus.   TB/3029
DIXON RYAN FOX: The Decline of Aristocracy in the
Politics of New York: 1801-1840. ‡ *Edited by Robert
V. Remini*   TB/3064
WILLIAM W. FREEHLING, Ed.: The Nullification Era: *A
Documentary Record* ‡   TB/3079
FELIX GILBERT: The Beginnings of American Foreign
Policy: *To the Farewell Address*   TB/1200
FRANCIS GRIERSON: The Valley of Shadows: *The Coming
of the Civil War in Lincoln's Midwest: A Contem-
porary Account*   TB/1246
FRANCIS J. GRUND: Aristocracy in America: *Social Class
in the Formative Years of the New Nation*   TB/1001
ALEXANDER HAMILTON: The Reports of Alexander Ham-
ilton. ‡ *Edited by Jacob E. Cooke*   TB/3060
THOMAS JEFFERSON: Notes on the State of Virginia. ‡
Edited by Thomas P. Abernethy   TB/3052
JAMES MADISON: The Forging of American Federalism:
*Selected Writings of James Madison. Edited by Saul
K. Padover*   TB/1226
BERNARD MAYO: Myths and Men: *Patrick Henry, George
Washington, Thomas Jefferson*   TB/1108
JOHN C. MILLER: Alexander Hamilton and the Growth of
the New Nation   TB/3057
RICHARD B. MORRIS, Ed.: The Era of the American Revo-
lution   TB/1180
R. B. NYE: The Cultural Life of the New Nation: 1776-
1801. † *Illus.*   TB/3026
FRANCIS S. PHILBRICK: The Rise of the West, 1754-1830. †
Illus.   TB/3067
TIMOTHY L. SMITH: Revivalism and Social Reform:
American Protestantism on the Eve of the Civil War
                                                             TB/1229
FRANK THISTLETHWAITE: America and the Atlantic Com-
munity: *Anglo-American Aspects, 1790-1850* TB/1107
ALBION W. TOURGÉE: A Fool's Errand. ‡ *Ed. by George
Fredrickson*   TB/3074
A. F. TYLER: Freedom's Ferment: *Phases of American
Social History from the Revolution to the Outbreak
of the Civil War. 31 illus.*   TB/1074
GLYNDON G. VAN DEUSEN: The Jacksonian Era: 1828-
1848. † *Illus.*   TB/3028
LOUIS B. WRIGHT: Culture on the Moving Frontier
                                                             TB/1053

American Studies: The Civil War to 1900

W. R. BROCK: An American Crisis: Congress and Reconstruction, 1865-67 ° △   TB/1283
THOMAS C. COCHRAN & WILLIAM MILLER: The Age of Enter-
prise: *A Social History of Industrial America* TB/1054
W. A. DUNNING: Essays on the Civil War and Reconstruc-
tion. *Introduction by David Donald*   TB/1181
W. A. DUNNING: Reconstruction, Political and Economic:
1865-1877   TB/1073
HAROLD U. FAULKNER: Politics, Reform and Expansion:
1890-1900. † *Illus.*   TB/3020
HELEN HUNT JACKSON: A Century of Dishonor: *The Early
Crusade for Indian Reform. ‡ Edited by Andrew F.
Rolle*   TB/3063
ALBERT D. KIRWAN: Revolt of the Rednecks: *Mississippi
Politics, 1876-1925*   TB/1199
ROBERT GREEN MC CLOSKEY: American Conservatism in
the Age of Enterprise: 1865-1910   TB/1137
ARTHUR MANN: Yankee Reformers in the Urban Age:
Social Reform in Boston, 1880-1900   TB/1247
WHITELAW REID: After the War: *A Tour of the Southern
States, 1865-1866. ‡ Edited by C. Vann Woodward*
                                                             TB/3066
CHARLES H. SHINN: Mining Camps: *A Study in American
Frontier Government. ‡ Edited by Rodman W. Paul*
                                                             TB/3052
VERNON LANE WHARTON: The Negro in Mississippi:
1865-1890   TB/1178

American Studies: 1900 to the Present

RAY STANNARD BAKER: Following the Color Line: *Ameri-
can Negro Citizenship in Progressive Era. ‡ Illus.
Edited by Dewey W. Grantham, Jr.*   TB/3053
RANDOLPH S. BOURNE: War and the Intellectuals: *Col-
lected Essays, 1915-1919. ‡ Edited by Carl Resek*
                                                             TB/3043
A. RUSSELL BUCHANAN: The United States and World War
II. † *Illus.*   Vol. I TB/3044; Vol. II TB/3045
ABRAHAM CAHAN: The Rise of David Levinsky: *a docu-
mentary novel of social mobility in early twentieth
century America. Intro. by John Higham*   TB/1028
THOMAS C. COCHRAN: The American Business System:
A Historical Perspective, 1900-1955   TB/1080
FOSTER RHEA DULLES: America's Rise to World Power:
1898-1954. † *Illus.*   TB/3021
JOHN D. HICKS: Republican Ascendancy: 1921-1933. †
Illus.   TB/3041
SIDNEY HOOK: Reason, Social Myths, and Democracy
                                                             TB/1237
ROBERT HUNTER: Poverty: *Social Conscience in the Pro-
gressive Era. ‡ Edited by Peter d'A. Jones* TB/3065
WILLIAM L. LANGER & S. EVERETT GLEASON: The Challenge
to Isolation: *The World Crisis of 1937-1940 and
American Foreign Policy*
                      Vol. I TB/3054; Vol. II TB/3055
WILLIAM E. LEUCHTENBURG: Franklin D. Roosevelt and
the New Deal: 1932-1940. † *Illus.*   TB/3025
ARTHUR S. LINK: Woodrow Wilson and the Progressive
Era: 1910-1917. † *Illus.*   TB/3023
GEORGE E. MOWRY: The Era of Theodore Roosevelt and
the Birth of Modern America: 1900-1912. † *Illus.*
                                                             TB/3022
RUSSEL B. NYE: Midwestern Progressive Politics: *A His-
torical Study of Its Origins and Development, 1870-
1958*   TB/1202
WILLIAM PRESTON, JR.: Aliens and Dissenters: *Federal
Suppression of Radicals, 1903-1933*   TB/1287
WALTER RAUSCHENBUSCH: Christianity and the Social
Crisis. ‡ *Edited by Robert D. Cross*   TB/3059
JACOB RIIS: The Making of an American. ‡ *Edited by
Roy Lubove*   TB/3070
PHILIP SELZNICK: TVA and the Grass Roots: *A Study in
the Sociology of Formal Organization*   TB/1230
IDA M. TARBELL: The History of the Standard Oil Com-
pany: *Briefer Version. ‡ Edited by David M. Chalmers*
                                                             TB/3071
GEORGE B. TINDALL, Ed.: A Populist Reader ‡   TB/3069
TWELVE SOUTHERNERS: I'll Take My Stand: *The South
and the Agrarian Tradition. Intro. by Louis D. Rubin,
Jr., Biographical Essays by Virginia Rock*   TB/1072
WALTER E. WEYL: The New Democracy: *An Essay on Cer-
tain Political Tendencies in the United States. ‡ Edited
by Charles B. Forcey*   TB/3042

Anthropology

JACQUES BARZUN: Race: *A Study in Superstition. Re-
vised Edition*   TB/1172
JOSEPH B. CASAGRANDE, Ed.: In the Company of Man:
*Twenty Portraits of Anthropological Informants.
Illus.*   TB/3047
W. E. LE GROS CLARK: The Antecedents of Man: *Intro.
to Evolution of the Primates.* ° △ *Illus.*   TB/559
CORA DU BOIS: The People of Alor. *New Preface by the
author. Illus.*   Vol. I TB/1042; Vol. II TB/1043
RAYMOND FIRTH, Ed.: Man and Culture: *An Evaluation
of the Work of Bronislaw Malinowski* ¶ ° △   TB/1133
DAVID LANDY: Tropical Childhood: *Cultural Transmis-
sion and Learning in a Puerto Rican Village* ¶
                                                             TB/1235
L. S. B. LEAKEY: Adam's Ancestors: *The Evolution of
Man and His Culture.* △ *Illus.*   TB/1019
ROBERT H. LOWIE: Primitive Society. *Introduction by
Fred Eggan*   TB/1056

EDWARD BURNETT TYLOR: The Origins of Culture. *Part I of "Primitive Culture."* § *Intro. by Paul Radin*   TB/33
EDWARD BURNETT TYLOR: Religion in Primitive Culture. *Part II of "Primitive Culture."* § *Intro. by Paul Radin*   TB/34
W. LLOYD WARNER: A Black Civilization: *A Study of an Australian Tribe.* ¶ *Illus.*   TB/3056

Art and Art History

WALTER LOWRIE: Art in the Early Church. *Revised Edition. 452 illus.*   TB/124
EMILE MÂLE: The Gothic Image: *Religious Art in France of the Thirteenth Century.* § △ *190 illus.*   TB/44
MILLARD MEISS: Painting in Florence and Siena after the Black Death: *The Arts, Religion and Society in the Mid-Fourteenth Century. 169 illus.*   TB/1148
ERICH NEUMANN: The Archetypal World of Henry Moore. △ *107 illus.*   TB/2020
DORA & ERWIN PANOFSKY : Pandora's Box: *The Changing Aspects of a Mythical Symbol. Revised Edition. Illus.*   TB/2021
ERWIN PANOFSKY: Studies in Iconology: *Humanistic Themes in the Art of the Renaissance.* △ *180 illustrations*   TB/1077
ALEXANDRE PIANKOFF: The Shrines of Tut-Ankh-Amon. *Edited by N. Rambova. 117 illus.*   TB/2011
JEAN SEZNEC: The Survival of the Pagan Gods: *The Mythological Tradition and Its Place in Renaissance Humanism and Art. 108 illustrations*   TB/2004
OTTO VON SIMSON: The Gothic Cathedral: *Origins of Gothic Architecture and the Medieval Concept of Order.* △ *58 illus.*   TB/2018
HEINRICH ZIMMER: Myth and Symbols in Indian Art and Civilization. *70 illustrations*   TB/2005

Business, Economics & Economic History

REINHARD BENDIX: Work and Authority in Industry: *Ideologies of Management in the Course of Industrialization*   TB/3035
GILBERT BURCK & EDITORS OF FORTUNE: The Computer Age: *And Its Potential for Management*   TB/1179
THOMAS C. COCHRAN: The American Business System: *A Historical Perspective, 1900-1955*   TB/1080
THOMAS C. COCHRAN: The Inner Revolution: *Essays on the Social Sciences in History* △   TB/1140
THOMAS C. COCHRAN & WILLIAM MILLER: The Age of Enterprise: *A Social History of Industrial America* TB/1054
ROBERT DAHL & CHARLES E. LINDBLOM: Politics, Economics, and Welfare: *Planning and Politico-Economic Systems Resolved into Basic Social Processes*   TB/3037
PETER F. DRUCKER: The New Society: *The Anatomy of Industrial Order* △   TB/1082
EDITORS OF FORTUNE: America in the Sixties: *The Economy and the Society*   TB/1015
ROBERT L. HEILBRONER: The Great Ascent: *The Struggle for Economic Development in Our Time*   TB/3030
ROBERT L. HEILBRONER: The Limits of American Capitalism   TB/1305
FRANK H. KNIGHT: The Economic Organization   TB/1214
FRANK H. KNIGHT: Risk, Uncertainty and Profit   TB/1215
ABBA P. LERNER: Everybody's Business: *Current Assumptions in Economics and Public Policy*   TB/3051
ROBERT GREEN MC CLOSKEY: American Conservatism in the Age of Enterprise, 1865-1910 △   TB/1137
PAUL MANTOUX: The Industrial Revolution in the Eighteenth Century: *The Beginnings of the Modern Factory System in England* ○ △   TB/1079
WILLIAM MILLER, Ed.: Men in Business: *Essays on the Historical Role of the Entrepreneur*   TB/1081
RICHARD B. MORRIS: Government and Labor in Early America △   TB/1244
HERBERT SIMON: The Shape of Automation: *For Men and Management*   TB/1245

PERRIN STRYKER: The Character of the Executive: *Eleven Studies in Managerial Qualities*   TB/1041
PIERRE URI: Partnership for Progress: *A Program for Transatlantic Action*   TB/3036

Education

JACQUES BARZUN: The House of Intellect △   TB/1051
RICHARD M. JONES, Ed.: Contemporary Educational Psychology: *Selected Readings*   TB/1292
CLARK KERR: The Uses of the University   TB/1264
JOHN U. NEF: Cultural Foundations of Industrial Civilization △   TB/1024
NATHAN M. PUSEY: The Age of the Scholar: *Observations on Education in a Troubled Decade*   TB/1157
PAUL VALÉRY: The Outlook for Intelligence △   TB/2016

Historiography & Philosophy of History

JACOB BURCKHARDT: On History and Historians. △ *Introduction by H. R. Trevor-Roper*   TB/1216
WILHELM DILTHEY: Pattern and Meaning in History: *Thoughts on History and Society.* ○ △ *Edited with an Introduction by H. P. Rickman*   TB/1075
J. H. HEXTER: Reappraisals in History: *New Views on History & Society in Early Modern Europe* △ TB/1100
H. STUART HUGHES: History as Art and as Science: *Twin Vistas on the Past*   TB/1207
RAYMOND KLIBANSKY & H. J. PATON, Eds.: Philosophy and History: *The Ernst Cassirer Festschrift. Illus.*   TB/1115
ARNALDO MOMIGLIANO: Studies in Historiography ○ △   TB/1288
GEORGE H. NADEL, Ed.: Studies in the Philosophy of History: *Selected Essays from History and Theory*   TB/1208
JOSE ORTEGA Y GASSET: The Modern Theme. *Introduction by Jose Ferrater Mora*   TB/1038
KARL R. POPPER: The Open Society and Its Enemies △
  Vol. I: *The Spell of Plato*   TB/1101
  Vol. II: *The High Tide of Prophecy: Hegel, Marx and the Aftermath*   TB/1102
KARL R. POPPER: The Poverty of Historicism ○ △ TB/1126
G. J. RENIER: History: *Its Purpose and Method* △ TB/1209
W. H. WALSH: Philosophy of History: *An Introduction* △   TB/1020

History: General

L. CARRINGTON GOODRICH: A Short History of the Chinese People. △ *Illus.*   TB/3015
DAN N. JACOBS & HANS H. BAERWALD: Chinese Communism: *Selected Documents*   TB/3031
BERNARD LEWIS: The Arabs in History △   TB/1029
BERNARD LEWIS: The Middle East and the West ○ △   TB/1274

History: Ancient

A. ANDREWES: The Greek Tyrants △   TB/1103
ADOLF ERMAN, Ed. The Ancient Egyptians: *A Sourcebook of Their Writings. New material and Introduction by William Kelly Simpson*   TB/1233
MICHAEL GRANT: Ancient History ○ △   TB/1190
SAMUEL NOAH KRAMER: Sumerian Mythology   TB/1055
NAPHTALI LEWIS & MEYER REINHOLD, Eds.: Roman Civilization. *Sourcebook I: The Republic*   TB/1231
NAPHTALI LEWIS & MEYER REINHOLD, Eds.: Roman Civilization. *Sourcebook II: The Empire*   TB/1232

History: Medieval

P. BOISSONNADE: Life and Work in Medieval Europe: *The Evolution of the Medieval Economy, the 5th to the 15th Century.* ○ △ *Preface by Lynn White, Jr.* TB/1141
HELEN CAM: England before Elizabeth △   TB/1026
NORMAN COHN: The Pursuit of the Millennium: *Revolutionary Messianism in Medieval and Reformation Europe* △   TB/1037

3

G. G. COULTON: Medieval Village, Manor, and Monastery
TB/1022

CHRISTOPHER DAWSON, Ed.: Mission to Asia: *Narratives and Letters of the Franciscan Missionaries in Mongolia and China in the 13th and 14 Centuries* △
TB/315

HEINRICH FICHTENAU: The Carolingian Empire: *The Age of Charlemagne* △
TB/1142

GALBERT OF BRUGES: The Murder of Charles the Good. *Trans. with Intro. by James Bruce Ross*
TB/1311

F. L. GANSHOF: Feudalism △
TB/1058

DENO GEANAKOPLOS: Byzantine East and Latin West: *Two Worlds of Christendom in the Middle Ages and Renaissance*
TB/1265

EDWARD GIBBON: The Triumph of Christendom in the Roman Empire (*Chaps. XV-XX of "Decline and Fall," J. B. Bury edition*). § △ *Illus.*
TB/46

W. O. HASSALL, Ed.: Medieval England: *As Viewed by Contemporaries* △
TB/1205

DENYS HAY: Europe: The Emergence of an Idea
TB/1275

DENYS HAY: The Medieval Centuries ○ △
TB/1192

J. M. HUSSEY: The Byzantine World △
TB/1057

ROBERT LATOUCHE: The Birth of Western Economy: *Economic Aspects of the Dark Ages.* ○ △ *Intro. by Philip Grierson*
TB/1290

FERDINAND LOT: The End of the Ancient World and the Beginnings of the Middle Ages. *Introduction by Glanville Downey*
TB/1044

MARSILIUS OF PADUA: The Defender of the Peace. *Trans. with Intro. by Alan Gewirth*
TB/1310

G. MOLLAT: The Popes at Avignon: 1305-1378 △ ○ △
TB/308

CHARLES PETIT-DUTAILLIS: The Feudal Monarchy in France and England: *From the Tenth to the Thirteenth Century* ○ △
TB/1165

HENRI PIRENNE: Early Democracies in the Low Countries: *Urban Society and Political Conflict in the Middle Ages and the Renaissance. Introduction by John H. Mundy*
TB/1110

STEVEN RUNCIMAN: A History of the Crusades. △
Volume I: *The First Crusade and the Foundation of the Kingdom of Jerusalem. Illus.*
TB/1143
Volume II: *The Kingdom of Jerusalem and the Frankish East, 1100-1187. Illus.*
TB/1243
Volume III: *The Kingdom of Acre and the Later Crusades*
TB/1298

FERDINAND SCHEVILL: Siena: *The History of a Medieval Commune. Intro. by William M. Bowsky*
TB/1164

SULPICIUS SEVERUS et al.: The Western Fathers: *Being the Lives of Martin of Tours, Ambrose, Augustine of Hippo, Honoratus of Arles and Germanus of Auxerre.* △ *Edited and trans. by F. O. Hoare*
TB/309

HENRY OSBORN TAYLOR: The Classical Heritage of the Middle Ages. *Foreword and Biblio. by Kenneth M. Setton*
TB/1117

F. VAN DER MEER: Augustine The Bishop: *Church and Society at the Dawn of the Middle Ages* △
TB/304

J. M. WALLACE-HADRILL: The Barbarian West: *The Early Middle Ages, A.D. 400-1000* △
TB/1061

History: Renaissance & Reformation

JACOB BURCKHARDT: The Civilization of the Renaissance in Italy. △ *Intro. by Benjamin Nelson & Charles Trinkaus. Illus.*   Vol. I   TB/40;   Vol. II   TB/41

JOHN CALVIN & JACOPO SADOLETO: A Reformation Debate. *Edited by John C. Olin*
TB/1239

ERNST CASSIRER: The Individual and the Cosmos in Renaissance Philosophy. △ *Translated with an Introduction by Mario Domandi*
TB/1097

FEDERICO CHABOD: Machiavelli and the Renaissance △
TB/1193

EDWARD P. CHEYNEY: The Dawn of a New Era, 1250-1453. * *Illus.*
TB/3002

G. CONSTANT: The Reformation in England: *The English Schism, Henry VIII, 1509-1547* △
TB/314

R. TREVOR DAVIES: The Golden Century of Spain, 1501-1621 ○ △
TB/1194

G. R. ELTON: Reformation Europe, 1517-1559 ** ○ △
TB/1270

DESIDERIUS ERASMUS: Christian Humanism and the Reformation: *Selected Writings. Edited and translated by John C. Olin*
TB/1166

WALLACE K. FERGUSON et al.: Facets of the Renaissance
TB/1098

WALLACE K. FERGUSON et al.: The Renaissance: *Six Essays. Illus.*
TB/1084

JOHN NEVILLE FIGGIS: The Divine Right of Kings. *Introduction by G. R. Elton*
TB/1191

JOHN NEVILLE FIGGIS: Political Thought from Gerson to Grotius: 1414-1625: *Seven Studies. Introduction by Garrett Mattingly*
TB/1032

MYRON P. GILMORE: The World of Humanism, 1453-1517. * *Illus.*
TB/3003

FRANCESCO GUICCIARDINI: Maxims and Reflections of a Renaissance Statesman (Ricordi). *Trans. by Mario Domandi. Intro. by Nicolai Rubinstein*
TB/1160

J. H. HEXTER: More's Utopia: *The Biography of an Idea. New Epilogue by the Author*
TB/1195

HAJO HOLBORN: Ulrich von Hutten and the German Reformation
TB/1238

JOHAN HUIZINGA: Erasmus and the Age of Reformation. △ *Illus.*
TB/19

JOEL HURSTFIELD, Ed.: The Reformation Crisis △
TB/1267

ULRICH VON HUTTEN et al.: On the Eve of the Reformation: *"Letters of Obscure Men." Introduction by Hajo Holborn*
TB/1124

PAUL O. KRISTELLER: Renaissance Thought: *The Classic, Scholastic, and Humanist Strains*
TB/1048

PAUL O. KRISTELLER: Renaissance Thought II: *Papers on Humanism and the Arts*
TB/1163

NICCOLÒ MACHIAVELLI: History of Florence and of the Affairs of Italy: *from the earliest times to the death of Lorenzo the Magnificent.* △ *Introduction by Felix Gilbert*
TB/1027

ALFRED VON MARTIN: Sociology of the Renaissance. *Introduction by Wallace K. Ferguson*
TB/1099

GARRETT MATTINGLY et al.: Renaissance Profiles. △ *Edited by J. H. Plumb*
TB/1162

MILLARD MEISS: Painting in Florence and Siena after the Black Death: *The Arts, Religion and Society in the Mid-Fourteenth Century.* △ *169 illus.*
TB/1148

J. E. NEALE: The Age of Catherine de Medici ○ △ TB/1085

ERWIN PANOFSKY: Studies in Iconology: *Humanistic Themes in the Art of the Renaissance.* △ *180 illustrations*
TB/1077

J. H. PARRY: The Establishment of the European Hegemony: 1415-1715: *Trade and Exploration in the Age of the Renaissance* △
TB/1045

J. H. PLUMB: The Italian Renaissance: *A Concise Survey of Its History and Culture* △
TB/1161

A. F. POLLARD: Henry VIII. ○ △ *Introduction by A. G. Dickens*
TB/1249

A. F. POLLARD: Wolsey. ○ △ *Introduction by A. G. Dickens*
TB/1248

CECIL ROTH: The Jews in the Renaissance. *Illus.*   TB/834

A. L. ROWSE: The Expansion of Elizabethan England. ○ △ *Illus.*
TB/1220

GORDON RUPP: Luther's Progress to the Diet of Worms ○ △
TB/120

FERDINAND SCHEVILL: The Medici. *Illus.*
TB/1010

FERDINAND SCHEVILL: Medieval and Renaissance Florence. *Illus.*   Volume I: *Medieval Florence*   TB/1090
Volume II: *The Coming of Humanism and the Age of the Medici*
TB/1091

G. M. TREVELYAN: England in the Age of Wycliffe, 1368-1520 ○ △
TB/1112

VESPASIANO: Renaissance Princes, Popes, and Prelates: *The Vespasiano Memoirs: Lives of Illustrious Men of the XVth Century. Intro. by Myron P. Gilmore*
TB/1111

Intellectual History & History of Ideas

HELLMUT WILHELM: Change: *Eight Lectures on the I Ching* △   TB/2019
HEINRICH ZIMMER: Myths and Symbols in Indian Art and Civilization. △ *70 illustrations*   TB/2005

Philosophy

G. E. M. ANSCOMBE: An Introduction to Wittgenstein's Tractatus. ° △ *Second Edition, Revised*   TB/1210
HENRI BERGSON: Time and Free Will: *An Essay on the Immediate Data of Consciousness* ° △   TB/1021
H. J. BLACKHAM: Six Existentialist Thinkers: *Kierkegaard, Nietzsche, Jaspers, Marcel, Heidegger, Sartre* ° △   TB/1002
CRANE BRINTON: Nietzsche. *New Preface, Bibliography and Epilogue by the Author*   TB/1197
MARTIN BUBER: The Knowledge of Man. △ *Ed. with an Intro. by Maurice Friedman. Trans. by Maurice Friedman and Ronald Gregor Smith*   TB/135
ERNST CASSIRER: The Individual and the Cosmos in Renaissance Philosophy. △ *Translated with an Introduction by Mario Domandi*   TB/1097
ERNST CASSIRER: Rousseau, Kant and Goethe. *Introduction by Peter Gay*   TB/1092
FREDERICK COPLESTON: Medieval Philosophy ° △ TB/376
F. M. CORNFORD: Principium Sapientiae: *A Study of the Origins of Greek Philosophical Thought. Edited by W. K. C. Guthrie*   TB/1213
F. M. CORNFORD: From Religion to Philosophy: *A Study in the Origins of Western Speculation* §   TB/20
WILFRID DESAN: The Tragic Finale: *An Essay on the Philosophy of Jean-Paul Sartre*   TB/1030
A. P. D'ENTRÈVES: Natural Law: *An Historical Survey* △   TB/1223
MARVIN FARBER: The Aims of Phenomenology: *The Motives, Methods, and Impact of Husserl's Thought*   TB/1291
MARVIN FARBER: Phenomenology and Existence: *Towards a Philosophy within Nature*   TB/1295
HERBERT FINGARETTE: The Self in Transformation: *Psychoanalysis, Philosophy and the Life of the Spirit* ¶   TB/1177
PAUL FRIEDLÄNDER: Plato: *An Introduction* △   TB/2017
ÉTIENNE GILSON: Dante and Philosophy   TB/1089
J. GLENN GRAY: The Warriors: *Reflections on Men in Battle. Intro. by Hannah Arendt*   TB/1294
WILLIAM CHASE GREENE: Moira: *Fate, Good, and Evil in Greek Thought*   TB/1104
W. K. C. GUTHRIE: The Greek Philosophers: *From Thales to Aristotle* ° △   TB/1008
G. W. F. HEGEL: The Phenomenology of Mind ° △   TB/1303
F. H. HEINEMANN: Existentialism and the Modern Predicament △   TB/28
ISAAC HUSIK: A History of Medieval Jewish Philosophy   JP/3
EDMUND HUSSERL: Phenomenology and the Crisis of Philosophy. *Translated with an Introduction by Quentin Lauer*   TB/1170
IMMANUEL KANT: The Doctrine of Virtue, *being Part II of the Metaphysic of Morals. Trans. with Notes & Intro. by Mary J. Gregor. Foreword by H. J. Paton*   TB/110
IMMANUEL KANT: Groundwork of the Metaphysic of Morals. *Trans. & analyzed by H. J. Paton*   TB/1159
IMMANUEL KANT: Lectures on Ethics. § △ *Introduction by Lewis W. Beck*   TB/105
IMMANUEL KANT: Religion Within the Limits of Reason Alone. § *Intro. by T. M. Greene & J. Silber*   TB/67
QUENTIN LAUER: Phenomenology: *Its Genesis and Prospect*   TB/1169
GABRIEL MARCEL: Being and Having: *An Existential Diary.* △ *Intro. by James Collins*   TB/310
GEORGE A. MORGAN: What Nietzsche Means   TB/1198

PHILO, SAADYA GAON, & JEHUDA HALEVI: Three Jewish Philosophers. *Ed. by Hans Lewy, Alexander Altmann, &Isaak Heinemann*   TB/813
MICHAEL POLANYI: Personal Knowledge: *Towards a Post-Critical Philosophy* △   TB/1158
WILLARD VAN ORMAN QUINE: Elementary Logic: *Revised Edition*   TB/577
WILLARD VAN ORMAN QUINE: From a Logical Point of View: *Logico-Philosophical Essays*   TB/566
BERTRAND RUSSELL et al.: The Philosophy of Bertrand Russell. *Edited by Paul Arthur Schilpp*
   Vol. I TB/1095; Vol. II TB/1096
L. S. STEBBING: A Modern Introduction to Logic △ TB/538
ALFRED NORTH WHITEHEAD: Process and Reality: *An Essay in Cosmology* △   TB/1033
PHILIP P. WIENER: Evolution and the Founders of Pragmatism. *Foreword by John Dewey*   TB/1212
WILHELM WINDELBAND: A History of Philosophy
   Vol. I: *Greek, Roman, Medieval*   TB/38
   Vol. II: *Renaissance, Enlightenment, Modern*   TB/39
LUDWIG WITTGENSTEIN: The Blue and Brown Books °   TB/1211

Political Science & Government

JEREMY BENTHAM: The Handbook of Political Fallacies: *Introduction by Crane Brinton*   TB/1069
KENNETH E. BOULDING: Conflict and Defense: *A General Theory*   TB/3024
CRANE BRINTON: English Political Thought in the Nineteenth Century   TB/1071
ROBERT CONQUEST: Power and Policy in the USSR: *The Study of Soviet Dynastics* △   TB/1307
EDWARD S. CORWIN: American Constitutional History: *Essays edited by Alpheus T. Mason and Gerald Garvey*   TB/1136
ROBERT DAHL & CHARLES E. LINDBLOM: Politics, Economics, and Welfare: *Planning and Politico-Economic Systems Resolved into Basic Social Processes*   TB/3037
JOHN NEVILLE FIGGIS: The Divine Right of Kings. *Introduction by G. R. Elton*   TB/1191
JOHN NEVILLE FIGGIS: Political Thought from Gerson to Grotius: 1414-1625: *Seven Studies. Introduction by Garrett Mattingly*   TB/1032
F. L. GANSHOF: Feudalism △   TB/1058
G. P. GOOCH: English Democratic Ideas in the Seventeenth Century   TB/1006
J. H. HEXTER: More's Utopia: *The Biography of an Idea. New Epilogue by the Author*   TB/1195
SIDNEY HOOK: Reason, Social Myths and Democracy △   TB/1237
ROBERT H. JACKSON: The Supreme Court in the American System of Government △   TB/1106
DAN N. JACOBS, Ed.: The New Communist Manifesto *and Related Documents. Third Edition, Revised*   TB/1078
DAN N. JACOBS & HANS BAERWALD, Eds.: Chinese Communism: *Selected Documents*   TB/3031
HANS KOHN: Political Ideologies of the 20th Century   TB/1277
ROBERT GREEN MC CLOSKEY: American Conservatism in the Age of Enterprise, 1865-1910   TB/1137
KINGSLEY MARTIN: French Liberal Thought in the Eighteenth Century: *Political Ideas from Bayle to Condorcet* △   TB/1114
ROBERTO MICHELS: First Lectures in Political Sociology. *Edited by Alfred de Grazia* ¶ °   TB/1224
JOHN STUART MILL: On Bentham and Coleridge. △ *Introduction by F. R. Leavis*   TB/1070
BARRINGTON MOORE, JR.: Political Power and Social Theory: *Seven Studies* ¶   TB/1221
BARRINGTON MOORE, JR.: Soviet Politics—The Dilemma of Power: *The Role of Ideas in Social Change* ¶   TB/1222
BARRINGTON MOORE, JR.: Terror and Progress—USSR: *Some Sources of Change and Stability in the Soviet Dictatorship* ¶   TB/1266

RELIGION

Ancient & Classical

J. H. BREASTED: Development of Religion and Thought in Ancient Egypt. *Intro. by John A. Wilson*   TB/57
HENRI FRANKFORT: Ancient Egyptian Religion: *An Interpretation*   TB/77
G. RACHEL LEVY: Religious Conceptions of the Stone Age and their Influence upon European Thought. △ *Illus. Introduction by Henri Frankfort*   TB/106
MARTIN P. NILSSON: Greek Folk Religion. *Foreword by Arthur Darby Nock*   TB/78
ALEXANDRE PIANKOFF: The Shrines of Tut-Ankh-Amon. △ *Edited by N. Rambova. 117 illus.*   TB/2011
ERWIN ROHDE: Psyche: *The Cult of Souls and Belief in Immortality Among the Greeks.* △ *Intro. by W. K. C. Guthrie*   Vol. I   TB/140;   Vol. II   TB/141
H. J. ROSE: Religion in Greece and Rome △   TB/55

Biblical Thought & Literature

W. F. ALBRIGHT: The Biblical Period from Abraham to Ezra   TB/102
C. K. BARRETT, Ed.: The New Testament Background: *Selected Documents* △   TB/86
C. H. DODD: The Authority of the Bible △   TB/43
M. S. ENSLIN: Christian Beginnings △   TB/5
M. S. ENSLIN: The Literature of the Christian Movement △   TB/6
JOHN GRAY: Archaeology and the Old Testament World. △ *Illus.*   TB/127
JAMES MUILENBURG: The Way of Israel: *Biblical Faith and Ethics* △   TB/133
H. H. ROWLEY: The Growth of the Old Testament △   TB/107
GEORGE ADAM SMITH: The Historical Geography of the Holy Land. ○ △ *Revised and reset*   TB/138
D. WINTON THOMAS, Ed.: Documents from Old Testament Times △   TB/85
WALTHER ZIMMERLI: The Law and the Prophets: *A Study of the Meaning of the Old Testament* △   TB/144

The Judaic Tradition

LEO BAECK: Judaism and Christianity. *Trans. with Intro. by Walter Kaufmann*   TB/823
SALO W. BARON: Modern Nationalism and Religion   JP/18
MARTIN BUBER: Eclipse of God: *Studies in the Relation Between Religion and Philosophy* △   TB/12
MARTIN BUBER: For the Sake of Heaven   TB/801
MARTIN BUBER: Hasidism and Modern Man. △ *Ed. and Trans. by Maurice Friedman*   TB/839
MARTIN BUBER: The Knowledge of Man. △ *Edited with an Introduction by Maurice Friedman. Translated by Maurice Friedman and Ronald Gregor Smith*   TB/135
MARTIN BUBER: Moses: *The Revelation and the Covenant* △   TB/837
MARTIN BUBER: The Origin and Meaning of Hasidism △   TB/835
MARTIN BUBER: Pointing the Way. △ *Introduction by Maurice S. Friedman*   TB/103
MARTIN BUBER: The Prophetic Faith   TB/73
MARTIN BUBER: Two Types of Faith: *the interpenetration of Judaism and Christianity* △   TB/75
ERNST LUDWIG EHRLICH: A Concise History of Israel: *From the Earliest Times to the Destruction of the Temple in A.D. 70* ○ △   TB/128
MAURICE S. FRIEDMAN: Martin Buber: *The Life of Dialogue* △   TB/64
GENESIS: The NJV Translation   TB/836
SOLOMON GRAYZEL: A History of the Contemporary Jews   TB/816
WILL HERBERG: Judaism and Modern Man   TB/810
ARTHUR HERTZBERG: The Zionist Idea   TB/817

ABRAHAM J. HESCHEL: God in Search of Man: *A Philosophy of Judaism*   TB/807
ISAAC HUSIK: A History of Medieval Jewish Philosophy   TB/803
FLAVIUS JOSEPHUS: The Great Roman-Jewish War, *with The Life of Josephus. Introduction by William R. Farmer*   TB/74
JACOB R. MARCUS: The Jew in the Medieval World △   TB/814
MAX L. MARGOLIS & ALEXANDER MARX: A History of the Jewish People   TB/806
T. J. MEEK: Hebrew Origins   TB/69
JAMES PARKES: The Conflict of the Church and the Synagogue: *The Jews and Early Christianity*   JP/21
PHILO, SAADYA GAON, & JEHUDA HALEVI: Three Jewish Philosophers. *Ed. by Hans Lewey, Alexander Altmann, & Isaak Heinemann*   TB/813
CECIL ROTH: A History of the Marranos   TB/812
CECIL ROTH: The Jews in the Renaissance. *Illus.*   TB/834
HERMAN L. STRACK: Introduction to the Talmud and Midrash   TB/808
JOSHUA TRACHTENBERG: The Devil and the Jews: *The Medieval Conception of the Jew and its Relation to Modern Anti-Semitism*   TB/822

Christianity: General

ROLAND H. BAINTON: Christendom: *A Short History of Christianity and its Impact on Western Civilization.* △ *Illus.*   Vol. I   TB/131;   Vol. II   TB/132

Christianity: Origins & Early Development

AUGUSTINE: An Augustine Synthesis. △ *Edited by Erich Przywara*   TB/335
ADOLF DEISSMANN: Paul: *A Study in Social and Religious History*   TB/15
EDWARD GIBBON: The Triumph of Christendom in the Roman Empire *(Chaps. XV-XX of "Decline and Fall," J. B. Bury edition).* § △ *Illus.*   TB/46
MAURICE GOGUEL: Jesus and the Origins of Christianity. ○ △ *Introduction by C. Leslie Mitton*
Volume I: *Prolegomena to the Life of Jesus*   TB/65
Volume II: *The Life of Jesus*   TB/66
EDGAR J. GOODSPEED: A Life of Jesus   TB/1
ROBERT M. GRANT: Gnosticism and Early Christianity. △ *Revised Edition*   TB/136
ADOLF HARNACK: The Mission and Expansion of Christianity in the First Three Centuries. *Introduction by Jaroslav Pelikan*   TB/92
R. K. HARRISON: The Dead Sea Scrolls : *An Introduction* ○ △   TB/84
EDWIN HATCH: The Influence of Greek Ideas on Christianity. § △ *Introduction and Bibliography by Frederick C. Grant*   TB/18
ARTHUR DARBY NOCK: Early Gentile Christianity and Its Hellenistic Background   TB/111
ARTHUR DARBY NOCK: St. Paul ○ △   TB/104
ORIGEN: On First Principles. △ *Edited by G. W. Butterworth. Introduction by Henri de Lubac*   TB/311
JAMES PARKES: The Conflict of the Church and the Synagogue: *The Jews and Early Christianity*   JP/21
SULPICIUS SEVERUS et al.: The Western Fathers: *Being the Lives of Martin of Tours, Ambrose, Augustine of Hippo, Honoratus of Arles and Germanus of Auxerre.* △ *Edited and translated by F. R. Hoare*   TB/309
F. VAN DER MEER: Augustine the Bishop: *Church and Society at the Dawn of the Middle Ages* △   TB/304
JOHANNES WEISS: Earliest Christianity: *A History of the Period A.D. 30-150. Introduction and Bibliography by Frederick C. Grant*   Volume I   TB/53
    Volume II   TB/54

Christianity: The Middle Ages and The Reformation

ANSELM OF CANTERBURY: Truth, Freedom and Evil: *Three Philosophical Dialogues. Ed., trans., and Intro. by Jasper Hopkins & Herbert Richardson*   TB/317

10

11

H. G. FORDER: Geometry: *An Introduction* △   TB/548

S. KÖRNER: The Philosophy of Mathematics: *An Introduction* △   TB/547

D. E. LITTLEWOOD: Skeleton Key of Mathematics: *A Simple Account of Complex Algebraic Problems* △   TB/525

GEORGE E. OWEN: Fundamentals of Scientific Mathematics   TB/569

WILLARD VAN ORMAN QUINE: Mathematical Logic   TB/558

O. G. SUTTON: Mathematics in Action. ○ △ *Foreword by James R. Newman. Illus.*   TB/518

FREDERICK WAISMANN: Introduction to Mathematical Thinking. *Foreword by Karl Menger*   TB/511

Philosophy of Science

R. B. BRAITHWAITE: Scientific Explanation   TB/515

J. BRONOWSKI: Science and Human Values. △ *Revised and Enlarged Edition*   TB/505

ALBERT EINSTEIN et al.: Albert Einstein: Philosopher-Scientist. *Edited by Paul A. Schilpp*   Vol. I TB/502
                                                                Vol. II TB/503

WERNER HEISENBERG: Physics and Philosophy: *The Revolution in Modern Science* △   TB/549

JOHN MAYNARD KEYNES: A Treatise on Probability. ○ △ *Introduction by N. R. Hanson*   TB/557

KARL R. POPPER: Logic of Scientific Discovery △   TB/576

STEPHEN TOULMIN: Foresight and Understanding: *An Enquiry into the Aims of Science.* △ *Foreword by Jacques Barzun*   TB/564

STEPHEN TOULMIN: The Philosophy of Science: *An Introduction* △   TB/513

G. J. WHITROW: The Natural Philosophy of Time ○ △   TB/563

Physics and Cosmology

JOHN E. ALLEN: Aerodynamics: *A Space Age Survey* △   TB/582

STEPHEN TOULMIN & JUNE GOODFIELD: The Fabric of the Heavens: *The Development of Astronomy and Dynamics.* △ *Illus.*   TB/579

DAVID BOHM: Causality and Chance in Modern Physics. △ *Foreword by Louis de Broglie*   TB/536

P. W. BRIDGMAN: Nature of Thermodynamics   TB/537

P. W. BRIDGMAN: A Sophisticate's Primer of Relativity △   TB/575

A. C. CROMBIE, Ed.: Turning Point in Physics   TB/535

C. V. DURELL: Readable Relativity. △ *Foreword by Freeman J. Dyson*   TB/530

ARTHUR EDDINGTON: Space, Time and Gravitation: *An Outline of the General Relativity Theory*   TB/510

GEORGE GAMOW: Biography of Physics Σ △   TB/567

MAX JAMMER: Concepts of Force: *A Study in the Foundation of Dynamics*   TB/550

MAX JAMMER: Concepts of Mass *in Classical and Modern Physics*   TB/571

MAX JAMMER: Concepts of Space: *The History of Theories of Space in Physics. Foreword by Albert Einstein*   TB/533

G. J. WHITROW: The Structure and Evolution of the Universe: *An Introduction to Cosmology.* △ *Illus.* TB/504